PHILOSOPHY AND ENVIRONMENTAL CRISIS

PHILOSOPHY
&
ENVIRONMENTAL CRISIS

edited by

WILLIAM T. BLACKSTONE

UNIVERSITY OF GEORGIA PRESS
ATHENS

Library of Congress Catalog Card Number: 73–90842
International Standard Book Number: 0–8203–0343–7

The University of Georgia Press, Athens 30602

Contents

PHILOSOPHY AND ENVIRONMENTAL CRISIS

Introduction

THESE PAPERS COMPRISE the Fourth Annual Conference in Philosophy, which was held at the University of Georgia 18–20 February 1971 and was sponsored by the Franklin College of Arts and Sciences of the University of Georgia and the Danforth Fund. Given the intense interest and the gravity of the problems centering around the use and abuse of environmental resources, and the challenge which these problems are generating for the value system of our society and of nations throughout the world, it was decided that the Fourth Conference would focus on what is now generally characterized as the "environmental crisis." Special emphasis was to be given, not so much to the factual data of the ecologist, but to the implications of that data for social, ethical, political, and legal values. Accordingly several nationally recognized philosophers were asked to join with philosophers at the University of Georgia in focusing on the conceptual and normative dimensions of this important current issue.

The stage for philosophical debate on the conceptual and normative implications of the environmental crisis was set by the initial lecture and discussion, given by Prof. Eugene Odum, an internationally recognized expert in the field of ecology who for years has been concerned with the need to develop an environmental ethic. Citing Aldo Leopold's essays on a "land ethic" written in the 1930s, Odum suggests that an ethic based on man-to-man relationships or on man-to-society relationships must be extended to include an ethical relationship between man and his environment. We must learn to think ecologically or "holistically" about the use of our environmental resources, Odum argues, if we are going to avoid self-destruction. Proper planning and management of environmental resources will require a revolution in the attitudes of human beings, one in which it is recognized that continued population growth, technology, and pollution can place such demands on the earth's finite resources that a quality human existence, if not human existence itself, is rendered impossible. The basis for such an "attitude revolution" must be, Odum argues, the development of an environmental ethic which will provide the necessary legal and economic incentives for change.

Following the ecologist Odum, seven philosophers presented papers on various philosophical aspects of the environmental crisis. In his contribution, Professor Feinberg argues that the protection of our environment is not only a matter of elementary prudence and of love for our children, but also a matter of justice, that is, of respecting the rights of unborn generations. His essay is an intricate analysis of the concept of a right and of the question of whether it is meaningful or conceptually possible to ascribe rights to animals, to species of animals, to plants, to fetuses, and to generations yet unborn. He recognizes that moral and legal rules presently exist for the protection of animals, but this leaves open the question of whether animals have rights which are correlative to the moral or legal duties which we have not to mistreat them. Not only ought we to treat animals humanely, but Feinberg argues such treatment is "owed" to animals. It is their "due." To withhold such treatment would be an injustice, and this means that animals have rights.

Logical conditions required for a being or entity to possess rights, Feinberg suggests, are that those beings or entities have interests, and hence, be capable of being represented; also, a right holder must be capable of being a beneficiary in his own person. The central criterion is what Feinberg calls the "interest principle," namely, that only the sorts of beings who can or do have interests are the sorts of beings who can or do have rights. Possession of interests presupposes at least rudimentary cognitive equipment, and since plants possess no such equipment, then they cannot have rights. The "interest principle" does permit us, however, to ascribe rights to infants, fetuses, and generations yet unborn on the grounds that interests can exert claims upon us before their possessors actually come into being. This, Feinberg notes, is analogous to the situation in which we respect the interests of dead men even after they as possessors of interests have ceased to exist. Unborn children then are among the sorts of beings of whom possession of rights can meaningfully be predicated because, even though they are temporarily incapable of having interests, it makes sense to protect their potential interests even before those interests have come into actuality.

This intricate analysis of the concept of a right and of the conceptual problems involving the meaningful predication of rights to various sorts of entities Feinberg connects to the problem of the environmental crisis. He argues that we owe it to future generations to pass on to them a world which is not "a used up garbage heap." This is a right of our remote descendants even though they are not yet present to claim a livable environment as their right, for there are plenty of proxies to speak on their behalf. The view that we may grant rights to remote and unidentifiable beings who are not yet in existence need not place us within the realm of obscure metaphysics, Feinberg argues. For whoever these human beings may turn out to be and however they may differ from us now, they will necessarily have interests, interests which we by our present action may affect, and this fact is all that is necessary, he suggests, in order to certify the coherence of our talk about their rights. Feinberg concludes that future unborn generations do have rights against us now and further that it is unfortunate indeed that human beings have run roughshod over our planet for several centuries as if there were no obligations to future generations or as if future generations have no rights against us now. His essay does much to clear away the conceptual confusion which has surrounded the notion of rights and the sorts of entities which are logically capable of possessing rights. His conceptual ground clearing is an important first step in the move to acknowledge the rights of unborn generations and consequently in the formulation of an environmental ethic.

Professor Blackstone argues that the basic causes of the environmental crisis are mistaken values and attitudes and that the resolution of this crisis will require a transvaluation of values. The latter will require, he argues, fundamental changes in our social, legal, and political institutions and in our "life-style." Blackstone recommends the adoption of the ecological attitude and his essay defines that attitude and explores the implications of ecological data for ethics in general and for a theory of rights in particular.

First he suggests that we need analysis and clarification of the key concepts used by ecologists, namely, stability, balance, homeostasis, and equilibrium in nature. The ecologist himself, Blackstone notes, admits that the meaning of these basic concepts varies, depending upon the variables in different contexts or ecosystems.

Their meaning becomes even more complicated when one speaks of human communities or ecosystems. What, for example, is the standard of environmental quality and population density which would define the meaning of a "homeostatic human population"? What is to be meant by an "ecological balance" when we are talking about the sociocultural needs of man? Blackstone points out that if these valuationally loaded terms—*homeostasis, equilibrium, balance,* and *stability*—are interpreted to mean largely man's biological and physical needs, then norms which are essential for man's state of well-being are left out of the picture. He warns us, then, not to carry the ecologist's value concepts over into a discussion of human populations without an adequate extension of those concepts. To extend those concepts, however, requires a general theory of value, which includes both an ethical theory and a theory of human rights.

If we are to speak of a homeostatic human society, Blackstone suggests, that notion must embrace several relevant and irreducible moral principles, which include at least the principles of utility and justice, for a homeostatic society must include not only conditions which maximize human welfare but also those in which welfare is properly or justly distributed among persons. Focusing primarily on the implications of ecology for a theory of rights, Blackstone argues that it is possible to conceptualize the right to a livable environment as an inalienable human right even though this right has not been so conceived in our political tradition. He suggests that the right to a livable environment can be conceived as an entailment of the basic rights to equality and freedom which are recognized in our political tradition.

Equality of treatment and equal freedom for each person in society now requires greater restrictions on the use of environmental resources, Blackstone argues. This is not to say, however, that all property rights must be denied and that the state must own all productive property, as the Marxists hold. If the right to a livable environment also were made a legal one, and if uniform anti-pollution laws were applied to all industries, then both the right to private property and the right to a livable environment could be seen as quite compatible with one another. Such compatibility, however, would require that industries operate within quite a different set of rules and attitudes toward the environment. Blackstone argues that this extension of government would not be equivalent to totalitarianism but rather is a necessary step to insure equality of rights, which is essential to a functioning democracy.

In his essay on the environmental results of technology, Professor Hartshorne points out that technology has made it possible for a large number of persons to enjoy the goods of life, greatly enlarging as well the numbers of persons who live with minimal or mediocre standards of living. This expansion of technological man has been at the expense of other forms of life, and Hartshorne points out that man faces limits beyond which his own extension is impossible or self-defeating. Although the addition of each person to the world adds value to the world, that person's existence also detracts from the value of the world; for he must compete with others for air, food, and water. Hartshorne holds that the West has many lessons to learn from Asia, especially the view that no form of life should be thought of as a mere means, for all forms of life are beautiful and good in themselves.

How much weight is to be put upon the preservation of nonhuman nature at the expense of the quantitative growth of man? Also, in terms of technological innovations, who is going to do without what in order to assure a certain qualitative existence for present and future life? These questions, Hartshorne acknowledges, are very difficult, and they call into question our entire system of values. He places these questions and our system of values within a metaphysical setting and makes this assertion: the root cause of destruction, suffering, and evil in the world is the cosmic principle of freedom. There is in Hartshorne's opinion an element of chaos at the heart of reality. That chaos amounts to the multiple freedom and self-determination of the many impinging upon the self-determination of each one. He implies that there is no final resolution of value choices and points out that technology magnifies both the risks and the opportunities of human choice.

Technology can be used to offset some of the harm which it itself produces. But within the metaphysical framework of freedom which he accepts, Hartshorne insists that we must develop a more balanced set of values which assigns human life its real place in the cosmos. This will require that we transcend a narrow patriotism, and develop a loyalty to both country and to mankind on the planet earth. In order to do this, we must develop more powerful international institutions which take the problems of mankind seriously.

In his contribution Professor O'Briant points out that in Western thought there have been two quite different ways of viewing man that can be characterized as "man apart from nature" and "man a part of nature." The former is basically the religious view in which man, although a part of the natural world, is also seen as a supernatural entity, made in the image of his Creator and conceived, in his most essential aspects, as transcending the bounds of nature. As a special creature of God, this view conceives of man as having dominion over other creatures.

The second view, that man is a part of nature, is basically the scientific view of man in which the notions of a spiritual Creator which presides over the natural world, a soul which survives death, and a supernatural realm are excluded. Here man is distinguished from other animals simply by the fact that he has a greater capacity to reason. O'Briant points out that this view is explicitly formulated by the zoologist Desmond Morris, who contends that, in a comparison of man with the apes, the only truly distinctive feature is the relative absence of bodily hair on man.

The religious view of man, in which man's true home is heaven, not the earth, has led to a careless and exploitative attitude toward the natural environment, O'Briant argues. This has been reinforced by what he calls the "frontier" attitude, that there is always an abundance of new territory and natural resources available for expropriation and exploitation.

Most of us, O'Briant believes, are committed to both of these world views—to both the scientific and the religious perspectives. The grounds for our actions are sometimes based on one perspective, sometimes the other. The crisis of our environment is in part caused by our ineffective dealing with these dichotomous world views, and the resolution of environmental problems, O'Briant argues, will require the formulation of a consistent and adequate view of man's relationship to nature.

Professor Rescher argues that we should not look upon the environmental crisis as a problem which can be "solved" but as a condition which will be a permanent feature of human experience on this globe and one to which we must adjust. He offers a rather pessimistic suggestion that the environment "has had it" and that we cannot simply return to the good old days of environmental purity. We can rectify some environmental problems; we can slow down the process of environmental degradation; but in the last analysis pollution and environmental degradation at some speed or another is a permanent condition of human affairs.

If we are to slow down the process of environmental degradation, Rescher suggests, then we must be willing to pay the price in terms of some of our ideological commitments. He argues that three major components central to the American ideology will have to go by the board: (1) The concept of material progress and of an ever-increasing quality of life must be curtailed. We must, in other words, deescalate our expectations. (2) The view that we are technologically omnipotent and can solve any problem through technology also must go. We must face the realities of finite resources and incapacities and become aware of accurate cost-benefit analyses in the use of environmental resources. (3) We must get rid of the millennial hankerings characteristic of a great deal of political rhetoric, the view that all of our problems can be solved if we simply put the right men in political office. This "pie in the sky" thinking we can no longer afford.

These changes in the American ideological perspective will help us carry on "a limited war in which an actual victory may well lie beyond our grasp." For the environmental crisis is more than a crisis which can be overcome by such changes. It is, Rescher argues, a permanent condition of things. Aside from piece-meal steps to slow it down, all of us will require "a large dose of cool realism tempered with stoic resignation."

Professor Burton who addresses himself to the value problems created by the unprecedented growth of human population—the population explosion or bomb—points out that it is a paradox of liberty that, in order to maximize liberty, we must agree to limit it. We impose these limitations upon ourselves through our moral, social, and legal institutions, and he points out that the principal task of political philosophy is to determine the limitations of human freedom within the state or political structure. In his opinion, adequate normative principles for the delimitation of human freedom are the irreducible principles of utility and justice, the former guiding us toward the maximization of goods and the latter providing a formula for the proper distribution of those goods.

With this normative structure sketched, Burton addresses himself to the problems created by the population explosion and states that the question is not whether we will reach zero population growth but when and for what reasons. Our finite biosphere can only support a limited number of humans. The question is whether our current world population, which is now approximately three and one-half billion and which will double in about thirty-five years, will be controlled by birth control or by death control. Surely, he argues, birth control is much more pleasant and humane than poverty, widespread hunger, starvation, disease, and an increased death rate.

Focusing upon the population growth in the United States, Burton suggests that we must change some of our basic attitudes. We must learn to want less, to consume less, and to waste less; also, we must, in the interest of equality of rights and a better quality of life for all, change our desire to have large numbers of children in each family. How is this to be done? Should government step in and censure parents who have more than two children? This effort at direct control of population, Burton feels, is foreign to our whole concept of government. The *raison d'être* of government in our political tradition is to prevent blatant injustice, but there is no blatant injustice in having more than two children. What could be done, he suggests, is moral persuasion, the effort to convince persons that a lowering of the birth rate will insure a better life for themselves and their children, and a shifting of tax burdens to discourage the having of large families.

Professor Gunter's contribution to this volume is a case study in environmental attitudes involving the "Big Thicket," a large and varied wildlife area of southeast Texas. As president of the Big Thicket Association, Professor Gunter has special interest in the preservation of this natural resource. (At present a bill to establish a Big Thicket National Park lies in congressional committee.) Gunter describes graphically the destructive acts which have reduced the Thicket to a remnant of what it was and treats it as a paradigm case of preurban or even preindustrial environmental degeneration. The beliefs and attitudes which have resulted in the abuse of this natural resource he characterizes as the "postulate of the environmental infinite" (the assumption that our environmental sources are infinite and that we can use our natural resources simply according to whim and caprice) and the "habit of inveterate atomism" (the position in which man conceives of himself as self-contained and atomlike, unrelated to nature as a whole). The end result of this atomism and the view that our natural resources are infinite, he declares, is one which suits our historical penchant for manipulation. These views of nature and man, Gunter declares, are connected, for in viewing nature as atomistically structured, infinite, and manipulatable, we view man concomitantly as an exploiter and manipulator.

The damage done to the Big Thicket has been sanctioned by this view of man and by the corresponding "use and possession" value system and legal system which stress a purely utilitarian concept of both ownership and use of natural resources, Gunter argues. "Nonmarket values," such as recreational and aesthetic uses of natural resources, have been for the most part excluded as playing an important role in our decisions on the use of environmental resources.

Gunter generalizes his conclusion concerning the Big Thicket. Different cultures, he argues, embody different world views; and different world views entail different views of man and his interaction with nature. What is needed both for the preservation of the Thicket and for the basis for a solution to the crisis of the environment is a change in our basic attitudes toward nature and man himself. Philosophy, he argues, can help us to construct a more adequate world view and a more adequate view of man.

All of these essays, focusing as they do on the conceptual and normative implications of ecological data, make significant contributions to the current debate on the environmental crisis. They constitute a philosophical prolegomena to the development of an environmental ethic.

WILLIAM T. BLACKSTONE

September 1973
Athens, Georgia

Environmental Ethic
and the Attitude Revolution

EUGENE P. ODUM

As HUMAN POPULATION GROWTH, technology, pollution, and demands on finite resources begin to tax the earth's capacity, the theory that man and environment are a whole must be put into practice if man is to avoid self-destruction. "Holism" in terms of planning and management requires a fundamental change in man's attitude toward his environment and, most important of all, an ethical basis for the necessary legal and economic incentives. The "environmental awareness movement," which began in the late 1960s is evidence that people's attitudes are changing rapidly, and so it would seem that the development of an environmental ethic is but a logical extension of general ethics.

Among recent ecologists who have considered the philosophical aspects of man and environment, the late Aldo Leopold, in his essays on the "land ethic"[1] wrote about three ethics: (1) religion as a man-to-man ethic, (2) democracy as a man-to-society ethic, and (3) a yet undeveloped ethical relationship between man and his environment. We would agree with Leopold that these three "ethics" are stages in the development of a general ethic in which man extends his thinking in stepwise fashion from man-to-man relationships to the totality of human existence. We can also present strong scientific and technological reasons for the proposition that such a major extension of the general theory of ethics is now necessary for human survival.

First, it would be prudent to define more precisely what is meant by "an environmental ethic" before presenting the case for considering it an extension of general ethics rather than a "new" ethic. In his earliest essay in 1933 Leopold wrote:

1. "The Conservation Ethic," *Journal of Forestry* 31 (1933): 634–643; "The Land Ethic," in *A Sand County Almanac* (New York: Oxford University Press, 1949).

When god-like Odysseus returned from the wars in Troy, he hanged, all on one rope, some dozen slave girls whom he suspected of misbehavior during his absence. This hanging involved no question of propriety, much less justice. The disposal of property was then, as now, a matter of expediency, not of right and wrong. Criteria of right and wrong were not lacking from Odysseus' Greece. The ethical structure of that day covered wives, but had not been extended to human chattels.

During the three thousand years which have since elapsed, ethical criteria have been extended to many fields of conduct, with corresponding shrinkages in those judged by expediency only. This extension of ethics is actually a process of ecological evolution. Its sequences may be described in biological as well as philosophical terms. An ethic, biologically, is a limitation on freedom of action in the struggle for existence. An ethic, philosophically, is a differentiation of social from anti-social conduct. These are two definitions of one thing. The thing has its origin in the tendency of independent individuals and societies to evolve modes of cooperation. The biologist calls these symbioses. Man elaborated certain advanced symbioses called politics and economies. Like their simpler biological antecedents, they enable individuals and groups to exploit each other in an orderly way. Their first yardstick was expediency. As the complexity of the human community increased expediency-yardsticks were no longer sufficient. One by one it has evolved and superimposed upon them a set of ethical yardsticks. The first ethic dealt with the relationship between individuals. Later accretions dealt with the relationship between individuals and society. Christianity tries to integrate the individual to society, Democracy to integrate social organization to the individual. There is yet no ethic dealing with man's relationship to land and to the nonhuman animals and plants which grow upon it. Land, like Odysseus' slave-girls, is still property. The land-relation is still strictly economic, entailing privileges, but not obligations. The extension of ethics to this third element in human environment is, if we read evolution correctly, an ecological possibility. It is the third step in a sequence. The first two have already been taken.

Civilized man exhibits, in his own mind, evidence that the third is needed. For example, his sense of right and wrong may be aroused quite as strongly by desecration of a nearby woodlot as by a famine in China. Individual thinkers, since the days of Ezekiel and Isaiah have asserted that the despoliation of land is not only inexpedient, but wrong. Society, however, has not yet affirmed their belief. I regard the present conservation movement as the embryo of such an affirmation.

Thus Leopold eloquently stated the case of a natural evolution of thinking about ethics, and he correctly predicted that the early "conservation movement" signaled the beginning of societal acceptance of an environmental ethic. What the conservationists of the 1930s could not have anticipated was the rapid rate of deterioration of man's environment that has accompanied the concentrated use of fuel power in cities and agriculture, the exponential growth of population that is supported and encouraged by this exploitation of fuel, and the shift from a technology based on making and using things that by and large can be recycled in nature to a technology based on the chemical conversion of natural products into poisons and nondegradable substances which can no longer be recycled by natural processes. It is the change in kind as well as the increase in amount of technology that places increasing stress on man's natural life-support system.

Just as the slaves of old eventually rose up and destroyed their masters, so will the damaged environment lead to destruction of man if he continues to treat the environment only as an expedient slave. Accordingly it matters not whether one takes the cynical viewpoint that man becomes ethical only when he has to or whether one believes that the goodness and wiseness in human behavior eventually surfaces. We can confidently expect that the decade of 1970 to 1980 will bring greater acceptance of the third ethic, because it must. In fact, we could argue with considerable logic that the progress man has made in formalizing the first two ethics will come to naught, unless the third and final component is accepted and put into legal and economic practice. Without a quality environment, there can be no organized society or quality individuals.

Cybernetics, the science of control theory, provides a convenient way to view the environmental problem as a whole. In cybernetic language a system such as a natural ecological system (ecosystem), or a human society, can exist in two general states: (1) a "transient" state in which the whole is growing or otherwise changing with time and (2) a "steady state" in which the system is maintained in an overall equilibrium. For the purposes of our analogy, we can think of the positive transient state as "youth" and the steady state as "maturity." There is, of course, the possibility of a negative transient state or "old age," which comes sooner or later to the individual, but which we assume need not come to the world ecosystem as a whole; at least, that possibility is not of immediate concern to society.

A growth or "youthful" stage is under the influence of what is called "positive feedback" in that each increase accelerates another increase, often in geometric progression (a doubling followed by a doubling, etc.). For the individual, the population, or for a new business, growth and positive feedback are necessary for survival. All organisms and living systems, in general, including nations of people, have an inherent tendency to grow, borne out of the necessity for survival. We see this in the development of a "growth ethic" in pioneer countries, such as the United States during the nineteenth and first half of the twentieth centuries. However, growth does not and cannot continue unrestricted because "negative feedback" control also comes into play, either due to some limitation imposed by the external environment or due to the action of an internal governor that brings about an orderly slowdown and establishes a set point at which growth in size stops (but this does not mean that growth in quality need stop). As systems become larger and more complex, more of the energy that it transforms must be fed back to maintain and control the quality of the intricate structure that has resulted from growth; quality maintenance replaces quantitative growth as "the strategy of survival" in the mature system. In summary then ultimate survival depends both on positive and negative feedback and on a set point control mechanism that prevents "overshoots," that is, damaging "boom-and-bust" oscillations that could cause the death of the system.

From this brief and elementary discourse on cybernetics, it can be seen that sooner or later transition from youth to maturity must be faced at all levels of life, whether they be cells, organs, teen-agers, society, or the ecosystem as a whole. In the individual there is a built-in governor in the form of a genetic code (a sort of computer) that first organizes growth, then slows it down, and then maintains optimum coordinated function in a state of maturity for a relatively long time. Viewing the United States as an ecosystem, we see that environmental constraints (depletion of resources, pollution, declining quality of living space, etc.) are beginning to provide negative feedback. As writers in the popular press are beginning to stress, this nation, whether we like it or not, is beginning to mature and stratify. Many of our current problems, both domestic and international, stem from our failure to face up to this fact. Thus, what was desirable in the youthful stage becomes undesirable in the mature stage. For example, high birth rates, rapid industrial growth and exploitation of unused resources are advantageous in a pioneer society. We can be justly proud of the fact that the United States has been able to grow and develop so well. However, as saturation levels are approached, all the "good" things become "bad" and the strategy of survival requires a shift to opposite poles, as for example, birth control, recycling of resources, regulation of land use, waste treatment, and so forth. Growth beyond the optimum becomes cancer. Cancer is an ever-present threat to any mature system and must be constantly guarded against. Unfortunately society has no built-in "genetic code" that automatically monitors the transition from youth to maturity. We have not yet agreed on optimum levels of population and energy transformation.

The theme of this essay, then, is that external environmental constraints will not be adequate negative feedback for society. So strong is the economic positive feedback of technological growth that overshoots seem inevitable if only external limits are involved. There must also be internal governors if transition is to be orderly and relatively free of cancerous excursions. Leopold's third ethic, or the extension of ethics to include man-in-environment relationships, must become an integral part of man's philosophy, if for no other reason than that such an extension provides the needed internal governor. Science can define reasonable levels and limits of growth and energy usage that are optimum for the quality of human existence, but ethics coupled with the legal and economic expediencies that derive from ethical behavior are absolutely necessary if we are to make the orderly transition to maturity.

Ethics and Ecology

WILLIAM T. BLACKSTONE

THAT THERE EXISTS today an environmental crisis of massive proportions is an unchallenged truth. No matter what aspect of the environment we focus on—water, air, land, industries, or cities —the problems of pollution, of the misuse and waste of resources, and of the improper distribution of those resources are massive. The crisis of the environment, however, involves not merely what some consider to be isolated and particular problems, such as the pollution of our lakes and rivers, the smog of our cities, and the devastating effect of pesticides on food chains; it involves a threat to life on this planet and certainly to the quality of that life. The ecological message is that there are no isolated problems and that we must learn to think holistically about our environment. Especially in man's present stage of technology, his alteration of the environment involves the total life system of the planet. Alteration can destroy and in fact is destroying in many cases the balance of nature which sustains that life system.

What are the causes of this crisis? The immediate causes are multiple: the misuse of technology to pollute, excessive proliferation of the human species, and ignorance of causal relationships in nature. But the basic underlying causes, I believe, are mistaken values and attitudes—the attitudes that we can exploit the environment without restrictions, that the production of goods is more important than the people who use them, that nature will provide unlimited resources, that we have no obligation to future generations to conserve resources, that continued increases in human population is desirable and that the right to have as many children as one wants is an inviolate right, that the answer to the problems of technology is more technology, and that gross differences and inequities in the distribution of goods and services are quite acceptable.

If this is true, if these values and attitudes are mistaken and are the root of the problems, then we need what Friedrich Nietzsche called for—a transvaluation of values. We do *not* need the kind of transvaluation that Nietzsche wanted, but we do need that for which ecologists are calling, that is, basic changes in man's attitude toward nature and man's place in nature, toward population growth, toward the use of technology, and toward the production and distribution of goods and services. We need to develop what I call the ecological attitude.

The transvaluation of values which is needed will require fundamental changes in the social, legal, political and economic institutions which embody our values. It may well require a fundamental change in what some call our life-style. Sound evaluative conclusions on resource use, however, require not only correct valuational premises but also correct empirical premises. We need both facts and values. The ecologist purports to provide those factual premises (along with some valuational premises), and I will begin this essay with a brief discussion of the status of the science of ecology. But my basic objective in this essay is to explore the implications of ecology and ecological data for ethics in general, for our traditional values, and for a theory of rights in particular.

THE STATUS OF THE SCIENCE OF ECOLOGY

What is the status of the science of ecology? I do not pretend to be able to answer this question adequately, but I think it must be asked and answered if one is to discuss intelligently the relationship between ecology and ethics in general or between ecology and a theory of rights. We must ask the status of the purported information and generalizations which the ecologist offers as knowledge, because they constitute crucial premises in arriving at conclusions about what we should do in connection with the use and care of our environmental resources—with how that use, and freedom of use, must be circumscribed. Perhaps the best way to do this is to see how ecologists themselves define their science and characterize the status of knowledge claims in this area.

Ecology has been defined by Odum as "the study of the structure and function of nature."[1] The word *ecology* is derived from the

1. Eugene Odum, *Ecology* (New York: Holt, Rinehart and Winston, 1963), p. 3.

Greek root *oikos* which means "house," and ecology is literally seen as a study of "houses or environments." In the sense of concern with the biology of groups of organisms and functional processes on land, rivers, and oceans, Odum helps to clarify what is embraced by the science of ecology by speaking of levels of organization. He asks us to think of a sort of biological spectrum which includes the following: protoplasm, cells, tissues, organs, organ systems, organisms, populations, communities, ecosystems, and the biosphere. Ecology as a science, he tells us, is concerned largely with the levels beyond the individual organism, that is, with populations, communities, ecosystems, and the biosphere. The biosphere is the biologically inhabitable soil, air and water constituting that part of the earth in which ecosystems can operate, and an ecosystem or ecological system is viewed as the population of a community, whether human or nonhuman, and the nonliving environment with which it functions.

Ecology attempts to provide us with information about regulatory mechanisms which operate at the population, community, and ecosystem level. These regulatory mechanisms are responsible for what might be called a state of homeostasis in the community or ecosystem level, just as certain body regulatory mechanisms are responsible for keeping a state of homeostasis in individuals.

Take two recent examples of man-made changes in the environment which some ecologists would argue have in fact upset a state of ecological homeostasis, the building of the Aswan Dam in the Upper Nile and the widespread use of DDT.[2] The Aswan Dam was built for a host of good purposes: to prevent flood damage, to provide electrical power, and to make available a supply of water for irrigation. Since the building of the dam, the annual flood of the Nile does not occur. The result of this is that the nutrients which the flood produced and carried to the eastern Mediterranean Sea are no longer so carried, and the annual bloom of phytoplankton no longer occurs. The food chain from vital plankton to zooplankton to fish has been broken, and the sardine fishery in the area which once produced over eighteen thousand tons per year now produces only about five hundred tons per year. Also

2. See William Murdock and Joseph Connell's discussion of this in their "All about Ecology," *Center Magazine* 3, no. 1 (January–February 1970): 56–63.

the stable lake which the dam has produced has permitted large populations of aquatic snails to develop. With larger human populations now living in the vicinity, the snails, serving as hosts of the larvae of a blood fluke which bores into humans, are infecting the liver and other organs of the humans living in this vicinity, causing the disease schistosomiasis. The ecologist points to these disturbances in the ecological balance when man introduces changes and makes us ask this question: Are the man-made changes worth the environmental cost?

The case of DDT is well-known. This pesticide is not readily broken down by microorganisms and therefore exists in the environment for a large number of years. Being very soluble in fats, it is taken up by organisms. It accumulates in the bodies of herbivores and becomes even more concentrated when herbivores are eaten by the carnivores. "The result is that the species at the top of the food chain end up with high doses of it in their tissues. Evidence is beginning to show that certain species of predators such as ospreys are being wiped out as a result of physiological debilities which lead to reproductive failure, all caused by cumulations of DDT," say Murdoch and Connell.[3]

Again the ecologist would have us be aware that the indiscriminate use of DDT as a pesticide can not only kill enemies but also friends of our environment. He forces us to consider whether the use of DDT is worth the price and if there is some way of using DDT which avoids the harmful effects of such use on our environment.

With this brief sketch, let us return to the question posed: What is the status of the science of ecology and how reliable is the information it provides? The ecologist attempts to provide models of how nature works and of the regulative mechanisms in nature. But ecologists recognize the complexity of their science and the difficulty of arriving at highly certain conclusions in their area. First, they recognize that ecology as a science is probably not older than forty years and that much of it is still in the stage of description.[4] Second, they recognize that ecology is the only field of biology which is not simply a matter of applied physics and chemistry.[5] Ecology is not only not independent of time or place,

3. Ibid., p. 57.
4. Ibid., p. 59.
5. Ibid.

but also each ecological situation is in fact different from every other one, having its own history. Some generalizations or law-like statements are possible but ecology as a discipline cannot provide us with the kind of broad generalizations provided by physics and chemistry.[6] Third, this means that only limited work can be done in the laboratory, for laboratory experimentation runs the risk of oversimplification of the ecosystem and of removing the elements which in fact determine how an ecosystem functions.

What can we infer from all of this? One ecologist straightforwardly states that the tentative understandings presently provided by ecology do not provide a sound basis for action by those who would manage the environment. I quote: "We submit that ecology as such probably cannot do what many people expect it to do; it cannot provide a set of 'rules' of the kind needed to manage the environment."[7] What the ecologist can do at this stage to assist in resolving our environmental crises is provide us with the right attitude, namely, a basic ecological attitude.[8]
Ecologists are generally more aware of the bad consequences of environmental manipulation and pollution than anyone else and whether we want to speak of their theories or statements as "knowledge" or as "wisdom" (a kind of ambivalence expressed by Joseph Connell), still the data and the perspective which they provide is the best we have at this time. As the science develops it will probably provide sounder theories and more reliable information required for decisions on how to manage the environment.

This note of caution about ecology as a science and the tentative state of the data and theories in this area, which the ecologist himself recognizes, does not uniquely apply to it. Information from any empirical science must have some degree of tentativeness about it. The degree may be higher in ecology. But such caution is important, for as Aristotle pointed out so well, ethics and politics deal with variables and although we cannot have absolute certainty in these areas of normative decision, we must base those decisions on the best data and theories. In the case of the proper

6. Ibid.
7. Ibid., p. 61.
8. Ibid.

use and management of our environment, tremendous consequences in terms of the quality of life are at stake.

THE ECOLOGICAL ATTITUDE

It would quite clearly be a major step forward if more persons adopted the ecological attitude, which embodies the explicit recognition that environmental changes will have repercussions and that environmental exploitation must be restricted. Analyzed further, the attitude incorporates (1) the acknowledgment that man can in fact cause irreversible changes in nature "since the genetic material of extinct species cannot be reconstituted";[9] (2) the awareness that our environmental resources are finite and nonrenewable and that we must learn to recycle scarce, nonrenewable resources; (3) the recognition that our environment has a limited capacity to absorb waste and pollution and to recycle it harmlessly. Beyond that point man's pollution of his environment can result in drastic alterations including changes in ocean productivity and weather; and (4) the acknowledgment that a finite world with finite resources cannot support an indefinitely expanding population or technology.

HOMEOSTASIS, STABILITY, EQUILIBRIUM

Most of us could agree with these basic points comprising the ecological attitude (though such an attitude is far from being universally accepted). But problems arise when we attempt to apply that attitude and to formulate environmental policy. There are two basic problems. One is the inadequacy or tentative state of much of the data provided by the ecologists and the relatively new state of ecology as a science, which were discussed earlier in this essay. Second, and this is not unconnected to this first point, we need analysis and clarification of certain key concepts employed by the ecologist, concepts which are central to his science, namely, "stability," "balance," and "homeostasis" in nature. The ecologist admits that the meaning of these terms varies, depending upon the kind of variables in different contexts. Stability in a

9. Ibid.

population, for example, may not mean mere numerical constancy. Some ecologists in fact suggest that numerical inconstancy is a criterion for stability. Also "a community or population might be considered stable because it does not change in response to a great deal of environmental pressure, or because it changes but quickly returns to its original state when the disturbing force is removed."[10] Ecologists themselves frequently admit that they are simply not sure what kind of prey-predator relationships provide stability of species.

The issue is more complicated when speaking of the human community, for these terms take on additional complexities and normative implications. The notions of stability, balance, and homeostasis in the human population involve value judgments about the quality of the environment and the quality of human life. Such concepts cannot be given a purely descriptive meaning. So we must ask: What is the standard of environmental quality and population density which would define the meaning of a homeostatic human population? What standards, in other words, are presupposed when we speak of an equilibrium between a human population and its environment? What is to be meant by an ecological balance when we are talking about the sociocultural needs of man? As Richard Peterson puts it, "the thirsty organism may satiate its need for liquid by drinking, but the need for power, wealth, knowledge, faith, and the like are apparently infinitely expandable."[11] What constitutes a balance when it comes to power? or wealth? or education? The normative problems here are vastly more complicated than those in reference to a balanced order among plants and animals in nature. Therefore, we must be very careful in moving from the use of concepts which were developed and utilized for the study of plant and animal communities to their use in human communities. Just as the notion of homeostatic balance when applied to plants and animals may not be directly applicable to human beings, so also the notion of an ecological balance within plant and animal communities may not be directly applicable to human communities. This is not to

10. Ibid.
11. Richard Peterson, "Technology: Master, Servant, or Model for Human Dignity" in Ervin Laszlo and Rubin Gotesky, eds., *Human Dignity: This Century and The Next* (New York: Gordon and Breach, 1970), p. 139.

deny that the ecological analogue is important in human affairs. But we must be wary of overextending that analogue. Or, perhaps better, we should be prepared to extend it properly to cover human affairs.

Let me clarify this further. If the valuationally loaded terms—homeostasis, equilibrium, balance, and stability—when applied to the human context are interpreted to mean largely man's biological and physical needs, then norms which are essential for man's state of well-being are left out of the picture. I have no objection to the use of these terms as basic normative premises for evaluations if they are conceived broadly enough to include all the components which are essential in assessing man's well-being. We must not ignore the psychological, social, and cultural factors which are so essential to what might be called a state of homeostasis in man. The solution to environmental crisis, in other words, involves not just physical or organic satisfaction and equilibrium but also what might be called cultural satisfaction and equilibrium.

We can put this in a different way: the basic needs of human beings must be fulfilled if they are to attain a state of satisfaction or balance or homeostasis, but the concept of need must be broad enough to include all of man's needs. Cameron's definition of need as "a condition of unstable or disturbed equilibrium in an organism's behavior, which . . . may arise directly from a change in the organism's relationship to its environment" seems to me broad enough.[12] It includes social, psychological, cultural, and aesthetic needs and roles. Expressed in terms of the notion of "codes" of a human being, this means, as Laszlo points out, that "the codes of the human being are not merely homeostatic norms, but also cognitive and aesthetic standards."[13]

I would add that those "codes" also must include certain basic moral and political standards. This is not to say that cultural equilibrium or homeostasis presupposes moral and political uniformity. Such equilibrium is compatible with a host of moral and political frameworks. But it is to argue that certain basic moral

12. Norman Cameron, *The Psychology of Behavior Disorders* (Boston: Houghton, Mifflin, 1947), p. 105; quoted by Ervin Laszlo, "Human Dignity and The Promise of Technology," in Laszlo and Gotesky, eds., *Human Dignity*, p. 106.
13. Laszlo, "Human Dignity," p. 106.

and political principles, those which insist upon certain basic freedoms and rights, are fundamental for such equilibrium. If those freedoms and rights are systematically violated, then social or cultural equilibrium is impossible.[14]

Let me now summarize the point I have been arguing. The questions posed earlier—what is the standard of environmental quality and population density which would define the meaning of a homeostatic human population? what is to be meant by an ecological balance when we are speaking of the sociocultural needs of man?—are very complex questions and they involve valuational premises which are beyond the distinct province of the ecologist. Those premises involve a general philosophy of man and a theory of value, including a theory of human rights.

Now it is well known that valuational premises which are universally acceptable are hard to come by. In fact some philosophers deny that the notions of certainty or knowledge are applicable to valuational statements. I reject this kind of skepticism. Some knowledge or probability is possible in the area of values (even in zones like ecology which involve complexities of both facts and values), and I agree with Helmut Buechner, head of the Office of Ecology at the Smithsonian Institution, and S. Dillon Ripley, secretary of the Smithsonian Institution, who state that "the humanist now has the responsibility of developing our understanding of values with relevance to the central ecological problems of our times."[15] What I will try to do in the following sections of this essay is to sketch such a value theory, which will help define the ecological notions of homeostasis, stability, equilibrium, or balance when we speak of the human population and its environment.

14. What is being said here is that moral and political frameworks which prevent the exercise of basic freedoms and rights violate the very nature of man as a rational and free being. Obviously, a defense of this argument would require a defense of the basic theory of man which underlies the argument and which underlies my view about the rights of man.

All of this is compatible with recognizing that the biological goals of man are genetically programmed and that cultural norms are empirically acquired or learned and that the latter are flexible. As Laszlo notes, one cannot choose not to be thirsty but one can choose not to be motivated toward a certain cultural norm ("Human Dignity," p. 107).

15. S. Dillon Ripley and Helmut K. Buechner, "Ecosystem Science as a Point of Synthesis," *Daedalus* 96, pt. 2 (Fall 1967) : 1196.

ECOLOGY AND ETHICS

We have already seen some of the difficulties confronting the concepts of homeostasis or stability as norms. Just as Aristotle recognized that the "golden mean" as a norm was highly relative, depending on the individual, his capacities, and circumstances, so also the norm of homeostasis or equilibrium is relative to different ecosystems. Furthermore, can we assume that all homeostatic or stabilized ecosystems are good or desirable? Unless one adheres dogmatically to a position of a "reverence for all life," the extinction of at least some species or forms of life and the generation of other forms may be seen as quite desirable. (This is parallel to the point frequently made by philosophers that not all "customary" or "natural" behavior is necessarily good.) Such a judgment requires, of course, a valuational perspective of some type and the question of the justification of that perspective immediately arises. Therefore if not all ecological homeostasis is desirable, which is? What fundamental—and justified—norms can we invoke to answer this question?

Let me offer at least a preliminary sketch of the problems involved in answering this question and then a tentative answer to it. Obviously, more than just the norms which are constitutive of what we have called the ecological attitude must be invoked because this question involves an assessment of ecological homeostasis itself. However, much depends on how far one stretches the meaning of homeostasis to include not only biological elements but cultural and moral ones as well.

Let us begin by asking this question: Is all value contingent on *man's* interest or preference? Even if we take Ralph Barton Perry's position that value is the object of any interest this would not be so.[16] There are entities or beings other than men—animals and perhaps gods. Part of the thrust of the ecologist may be to get us to expand our narrow man-centered evaluations and see things, if not from the viewpoint of gods, at least from the viewpoint of "nature." However, even if all value is man-dependent and even if the concept of value and valuation is meaningless apart

16. Ralph Barton Perry, *Realms of Value* (Cambridge, Mass.: Harvard University Press, 1954).

from human beings and their perspectives, attitudes, and preferences (which is at the very least a questionable assumption), still this purely man-oriented perspective requires consideration of *all* men and the conditions for maximizing their values. This in turn surely requires a careful calculation of the consequences of any alteration of the environment or of any destruction of life. Such alteration or destruction may enhance the quality of human life and maximize human welfare. On the other hand it may do just the opposite and irreversibly damage the environment. Disadvantages or value destruction as well as benefits or value construction must be carefully weighed. And yet it is obvious that very little careful calculation is being done on either national or international levels.

The underlying value premise in what has been said is plainly the public interest, with "public" broadly construed. Public interest here includes optimum living conditions for all human beings, those now existing and those yet to come. One should not be surprised that this sounds very much like Jeremy Bentham and John Stuart Mill—extended and "ecologized" to be sure.

But mere utility or optimum living and environmental conditions is not enough. This concern for human welfare all over the globe must also be conjoined with another fundamental value, that of justice and the intrinsic worth and dignity of all human life. (I am not prepared to say "all life.") In disagreement with Bentham and Mill, I do not think that justice, or norms which invoke the concept of rights, can be subsumed under the principle of utility or reduced to purely utilitarian considerations. We cannot explore this issue or that of value reductionism in ethics here. Let me simply, and dogmatically in this context, state that the norm of justice is separate and independent of the norm of utility —no matter how *useful* the norm of justice. This means that the notion of a homeostatic society, if we are to use this language to speak of the social and moral realm, must embrace several relevant and irreducible moral principles, at least the principles of utility and justice. We must be concerned not merely with a human and natural environment which maximizes human welfare but one in which that welfare is properly or justly distributed among men. This, of course, raises the question of the meaning of justice, which is a long story for another occasion. But let me re-peat that justice as a norm, with all its attendant difficulties and perplexities, must be included along with utility or maximum human welfare as a fundamental norm in assessing or, indeed, defining a homeostatic society. Man has done poorly enough in embracing the norm of justice without all of the new and increas-ing ecological information. With this data, the problem of justice and its application, nationally and internationally, becomes even more complex and difficult. Since utility and justice as norms are not reducible one to the other and in fact may conflict on occa-sion, difficult moral problems will arise where decisions must be made on how our environmental resources are to be used and allocated. Justice or the proper distribution of resources may have to be sacrificed on occasion for the sake of greater utility; on other occasions it might be proper to sacrifice some degree of utility for just distribution of resources. Such decisions, difficult though they may be, cannot be avoided, for morally relevant considerations are many and complex, and there are no self-applying rules.

This is not the place to state and defend a total ethic, but the norms of utility and justice—perhaps others—provide what I be-lieve to be an objective set of values. The objectivity and universal nature of these norms hold, even though there are difficulties in applying them and even though there are relativities of content when applied in different contexts. The anthropologist Clyde Kluckhohn states this extremely well:

All cultures constitute so many somewhat distinct answers to essentially the same questions posed by human biology and by the generalities of the human situation. . . . Every society's pattern for living must provide approved and sanctioned ways for dealing with such universal circumstances as the existence of two sexes; the helplessness of infants; the need for satisfaction of the elementary biological requirements such as food, warmth, and sex; and presence of individuals of different ages and of differing physical and other capacities. The basic similarities in human biology the world over are vastly more massive than the variations. Equally, there are certain necessities in social life for this kind of animal, regardless of where that life is carried on or in what culture. Cooperation to obtain subsistence and for other ends requires a certain minimum of reciprocal behavior, of a standard system of communication, and, indeed, of mutually accepted values."[17]

Kluckhohn's thesis I believe to be corect. Men everywhere have similar biological, psychological, and social needs, and many of the norms and values which man has developed in order to satisfy these basic needs are cross-culturally accepted norms. Sure, there is cultural relativity, but there are also structural regularities which underlie all cultures or human ecosystems. Kluckhohn goes so far as to suggest that that structural regularity "may well be the same urge for conformance to form and pattern which appears to be a property of all nature."[18] This suggests that ecosystem thinking, the emphasis on organization and structural relationships on the organic and suborganic level, should be extended to the sociocultural level. Human populations have adapted to their environment by invoking a variety of norms and systems of organization, in particular the fundamental norms of justice and utility. What is now required is that human ecosystems employ these norms to adapt to a problem perhaps more fundamental than those mentioned by Kluckhohn, the necessity of conserving and preserving the environmental conditions upon which our lives and the quality of our lives depend.

Let me summarize the basic point I have argued. The ecological attitude as defined above requires nothing new in terms of moral principles. It does require a more sophisticated and careful assessment of actions and their effects on the environment than has been done in the past. In other words, it requires a more sophisticated application of the principle of utility. And this application must be linked to the application of the principle of justice; for unjust societies cannot properly be seen as homeostatic (in the moral sense), no matter how overtly stable they may seem. Not merely maximum utility or resource use (with necessary recycling) but

17. Alfred Kroeber and Clyde Kluckhohn, *Culture: A Critical Review of Concepts and Definitions*, Papers of The Peabody Museum, Harvard University, vol. 47, no. 1 (1952): 175.
18. Ibid.

the proper distribution of those resources is essential to a quality human life for all.

ECOLOGY AND RIGHTS

Up to this point I have spoken in general terms about the implications of ecology for ethics. I want now to focus on one segment of morality—that of justice and rights—and the possible implications of ecological data for this segment.

Much has been said about the right to a decent or livable environment. In his 22 January 1970 state of the union address, President Nixon stated: "The great question of the seventies is, shall we surrender to our surroundings, or shall we make our peace with Nature and begin to make the reparations for the damage we have done to our air, our land, and our water? . . . Clean air, clean water, open spaces—these would once again be the birthright of every American; if we act now, they can be." It seems, though, that the use of the term *right* by President Nixon, under the rubric of a "birthright" to a decent environment, is not a strict sense of the term. That is, he does not use this term to indicate that one has or should have either a legal right or a moral right to a decent environment. Rather he is pointing to the fact that in the past our environmental resources have been so abundant that all Americans did in fact inherit a livable environment, and it would be *desirable* that this state of affairs again be the case. Pollution and the exploitation of our environment is precluding this kind of inheritance.

Few would challenge the desirability of such a state of affairs or of such a "birthright." What we want to ask is whether the right to a decent environment can or ought to be considered a right in a stricter sense, either in a legal or moral sense. In contrast to a merely desirable state of affairs, a right entails a correlative duty or obligation on the part of someone or some group to accord one a certain mode of treatment or to act in a certain way.[19] Desirable states of affairs do not entail such correlative duties or obligations.

19. This is a dogmatic assertion in this context. I am aware that some philosophers deny that rights and duties are correlative. Strictly interpreted this correlativity thesis is false, I believe. There are duties for which there are no correlative rights. But space does not permit discussion of this question here.

THE RIGHT TO A LIVABLE ENVIRONMENT
AS A HUMAN RIGHT

Let us first ask whether the right to a livable environment can properly be considered to be a human right. For the purposes of this paper, however, I want to avoid raising the more general question of whether there are any human rights at all. Some philosophers do deny that any human rights exist.[20] In two recent papers I have argued that human rights do exist (even though such rights may properly be overridden on occasion by other morally relevant reasons) and that they are universal and inalienable (although the actual exercise of such rights on a given occasion is alienable).[21] My argument for the existence of universal human rights rests, in the final analysis, on a theory of what it means to be human, which specifies the capacities for rationality and freedom as essential, and on the fact that there are no relevant grounds for excluding any human from the opportunity to develop and fulfill his capacities (rationality and freedom) as a human. This is not to deny that there are criteria which justify according human rights in quite different ways or with quite different modes of treatment for different persons, depending upon the nature and degree of such capacities and the existing historical and environmental circumstances.

If the right to a livable environment were seen as a basic and inalienable human right, this could be a valuable tool (both inside and outside of legalistic frameworks) for solving some of our environmental problems, both on a national and on an international basis. Are there any philosophical and conceptual difficulties in treating this right as an inalienable human right? Traditionally we have not looked upon the right to a decent environment as a human right or as an inalienable right. Rather, inalienable human or natural rights have been conceived in somewhat different terms; equality, liberty, happiness, life, and property. However, might it not be possible to view the right to a

---

20. See Kai Nielsen's "Scepticism and Human Rights," *Monist* 52, no. 4 (1968): 571–594.
21. See my "Equality and Human Rights," *Monist* 52, no. 4 (1968): 616–639 and my "Human Rights and Human Dignity," in Laszlo and Gotesky, eds., *Human Dignity*.

livable environment as being entailed by, or as constitutive of, these basic human or natural rights recognized in our political tradition? If human rights, in other words, are those rights which each human possesses in virtue of the fact that he is human and in virtue of the fact that those rights are essential in permitting him to live a human life (that is, in permitting him to fulfill his capacities as a rational and free being), then might not the right to a decent environment be properly categorized as such a human right? Might it not be conceived as a right which has emerged as a result of changing environmental conditions and the impact of those conditions on the very possibility of human life and on the possibility of the realization of other rights such as liberty and equality?[22] Let us explore how this might be the case.

Given man's great and increasing ability to manipulate the environment, and the devastating effect this is having, it is plain that new social institutions and new regulative agencies and procedures must be initiated on both national and international levels to make sure that the manipulation is in the public interest. It will be necessary, in other words, to restrict or stop some practices and the freedom to engage in those practices. Some look upon such additional state planning, whether national or international, as unnecessary further intrusion on man's freedom. Freedom is, of course, one of our basic values, and few would deny that excessive state control of human action is to be avoided. But such restrictions on individual freedom now appear to be necessary in the interest of overall human welfare and the rights and freedoms of *all* men. Even John Locke with his stress on freedom as an inalienable right recognized that this right must be construed so that it is consistent with the equal right to freedom of others. The whole point of the state is to restrict unlicensed freedom and to provide the conditions for equality of rights for all. Thus it seems to be perfectly consistent with Locke's view and, in general, with the

22. Almost forty years ago, Aldo Leopold stated that "there is as yet no ethic dealing with man's relationship to land and to the non-human animals and plants which grow upon it. Land, like Odysseus' slave girls, is still property. The land relation is still strictly economic entailing privileges but not obligations." (See Leopold's "The Conservation Ethic," *Journal of Forestry* 31, no. 6 (October 1933): 634–643. Although some important changes have occurred since he wrote this, no systematic ethic or legal structure has been developed to socialize or institutionalize the obligation to use land properly.

views of the founding fathers of this country to restrict certain rights or freedoms when it can be shown that such restriction is necessary to insure the equal rights of others. If this is so, it has very important implications for the rights to freedom and to property. These rights, perhaps properly seen as inalienable (though this is a controversial philosophical question), are not properly seen as unlimited or unrestricted. When values which we hold dear conflict (for example, individual or group freedom and the freedom of all, individual or group rights and the rights of all, and individual or group welfare and the welfare of the general public) something has to give; some priority must be established. In the case of the abuse and waste of environmental resources, less individual freedom and fewer individual rights for the sake of greater public welfare and equality of rights seem justified. What in the past had been properly regarded as freedoms and rights (given what seemed to be unlimited natural resources and no serious pollution problems) can no longer be so construed, at least not without additional restrictions. We must recognize both the need for such restrictions and the fact that none of our rights can be realized without a livable environment. Both public welfare and equality of rights now require that natural resources not be used simply according to the whim and caprice of individuals or simply for personal profit. This is not to say that all property rights must be denied and that the state must own all productive property, as the Marxist argues. It is to insist that those rights be qualified or restricted in the light of new ecological data and in the interest of the freedom, rights, and welfare of all.

The answer then to the question, Is the right to a livable environment a human right? is yes. Each person has this right qua being human and because a livable environment is essential for one to fulfill his human capacities. And given the danger to our environment today and hence the danger to the very possibility of human existence, access to a livable environment must be conceived as a right which imposes upon everyone a correlative moral obligation to respect.[23]

---

23. The right to a livable environment might itself entail other rights, for example, the right to population control. Population control is obviously essential for quality human existence. This issue is complex and deserves a separate essay, but I believe that the moral framework explicated above pro-

THE RIGHT TO A LIVABLE ENVIRONMENT AS A LEGAL RIGHT

If the right to a decent environment is to be treated as a legal right, then obviously what is required is some sort of legal framework which gives this right a legal status. Such legal frameworks have been proposed. Sen. Gaylord Nelson, originator of Earth Day, recently proposed a Constitutional Amendment guaranteeing every American an inalienable right to a decent environment.[24] Others want to formulate an entire "environmental bill of rights" to assist in solving our pollution problems. Such a bill of rights or a constitutional revision would provide a legal framework for the enforcement of certain policies bearing on environmental issues. It would also involve the concept of "legal responsibility" for acts which violate those rights. Such legal responsibility is beginning to be enforced in the United States. President Nixon on 23 December 1970 signed an executive order requiring industries to obtain federal permits before dumping pollutants. He issued the order not under the authority of new legislation but under the Refuse Act of 1899, which was originally designed to control discharges in connection with dredging and water construction operations but now has been broadened by Supreme Court decisions to cover pollution resulting from industrial operations. (The extension of this act is similar to my suggestion above, namely, the extension of the constitutional rights to equality, liberty, and property to include the right to a livable environment.)

Others propose that the right to a decent environment also be a cardinal tenet of international law. Pollution is not merely a national problem but an international one. The population of the entire world is affected by it, and a body of international law, which includes the right to a decent environment and the accompanying policies to save and preserve our environmental resources, would be an even more effective tool than such a framework at the national level. Of course, one does not have to be reminded of the problems involved in establishing international law and in eliciting obedience to it. Conflicts between nations are still settled more by force than by law or persuasion. The record of the

---

vides the grounds for treating population control both as beneficial and as moral.

24. *Newsweek*, 4 May 1970, p. 26.

United Nations attests to this fact. In the case of international conflict over environmental interests and the use of the environment, the possibility of international legal resolution, at least at this stage of history, is somewhat remote; for the body of enforceable international law on this topic is meager indeed. This is not to deny that this is the direction in which we should (and must) move.

A good case can be made for the view that not all moral or human rights should be legal rights and that not all moral rules should be legal rules. It may be argued that any society which covers the whole spectrum of man's activities with legally enforceable rules minimizes his freedom and approaches totalitarianism. There is this danger. But just as we argued that certain traditional rights and freedoms are properly restricted in order to insure the equal rights and welfare of all, so also it can plausibly be argued that the human right to a livable environment should become a legal one in order to assure that it is properly respected. Given the magnitude of the present dangers to the environment and to the welfare of all humans, and the ingrained habits and rules, or lack of rules, which permit continued waste, pollution, and destruction of our environmental resources, the legalized status of the right to a livable environment seems both desirable and necessary.

Such a legal right would provide a tool for pressing environmental transgressions in the courts. At the present the right to a livable environment, even if recognized as a human right, is not generally recognized as a legal one. One cannot sue individuals or corporations for polluting the environment, if the pollution harms equally every member of a community. One can sue such individuals or corporations if they damage one's private property but not if they damage the public environment. It is true that public officials have a legal standing in cases of generalized pollution, but unfortunately they have done little to exercise that standing.

Since public officials are failing to take steps to protect the environment, Joseph Sax, professor of law at the University of Michigan, argues that the right to take environmental disputes to court must be obtained as a right of private citizens: "The No. 1 legal priority of those concerned with governmental protection now is that the old restraints of the public nuisance doctrine and other archaic rules be rooted out of the law and be replaced with the recognition of every citizen's opportunity to enforce at law the right to a decent environment."[25] Sax himself drafted a model environmental law which was presented to the Michigan legislature, which "empowered any person or organization to sue any private or public body and to obtain a court order restraining conduct that is likely to pollute, impair, or destroy the air, water, or other material resources or the public trust therein."[26] This bill has now become law, and a similar bill is pending in the U.S. Congress, having been introduced by Senators McGovern and Hart and Representative Udall. I concur with Sax that this law, which provides an enforceable right to a decent environment and which places the burden of proof on a polluter or would-be polluter to show that his action affecting the environment is consistent with public health and welfare, "offers the promise of a dramatic legal break-through in the effort to protect environmental quality."[27] Although it may add to the clogged conditions of the courts, it should also have the effect of encouraging careful planning of activities which affect the environment.

The history of government, in this country and elsewhere, has been that of the gradual demise of a laissez-faire philosophy of government. Few deny that there are areas of our lives where government should not and must not intrude. In fact, what we mean by a totalitarian government is one which exceeds its proper bounds and attempts to control nearly all human activities. But in some areas of human life, it has been seen that the "keep-government-out-of-it" attitude just will not work. The entire quality of life in a society is determined by the availability and distribution of goods and services in such vital areas as education, housing, medical treatment, legal treatment, and so on. In the field of education, for example, we have seen the need for compulsory education and, more recently, for unitary school systems in order to provide equality of educational opportunity. In the area of medical treatment it is plain that we need "new systems of health ser-

25. Joseph Sax, "Environment in The Courtroom," *Saturday Review*, 3 October 1970, p. 56.
26. Ibid.
27. Ibid.

vice delivery that stress better distribution, accessibility, cost containment and increased quality without sacrificing quality."[28] Dr. John Knowles, former president of the American Medical Association argues that we cannot expect this from a system in which the free market economy sets the fees of physicians. Nor can we expect it from the AMA which some characterize as an "ogre in the form of a vast and powerful trade union interested only in economic advancement of its members."[29] Government must step in to provide these vital health services.

In the same way, it is essential that government step in to prevent the potentially dire consequences of industrial pollution and the waste of environmental resources. Such government regulations need not mean the death of the free enterprise system. The right to private property can be made compatible with the right to a livable environment, for if uniform antipollution laws were applied to all industries, then both competition and private ownership could surely continue. But they would continue within a quite different set of rules and attitudes toward the environment. This extension of government would not be equivalent to totalitarianism. In fact it is necessary to insure equality of rights and freedom, which is essential to a democracy.

ECOLOGY AND ECONOMIC RIGHTS

We suggested above that it is necessary to qualify or restrict economic or property rights in the light of new ecological data and in the interest of the freedom, rights, and welfare of all. In part, this suggested restriction is predicated on the assumption that we cannot expect private business to provide solutions to the multiple pollution problems for which they themselves are responsible. Some companies have taken measures to limit the polluting effect of their operations, and this is an important move. But we are deluding ourselves if we think that private business can function as its own pollution police. This is so for several reasons: the primary objective of private business is economic profit. Stockholders do

28. John Knowles, "Where Doctors Fail," *Saturday Review*, 27 August 1970, p. 63.
29. Ibid.

not ask of a company, "Have you polluted the environment and lowered the quality of the environment for the general public and for future generations?" Rather they ask, "How high is the annual dividend and how much higher is it than the year before?" One can hardly expect organizations whose basic norm is economic profit to be concerned in any great depth with the long-range effects of their operations upon society and future generations or concerned with the hidden cost of their operations in terms of environmental quality to society as a whole. Second, within a free enterprise system companies compete to produce what the public wants at the lowest possible cost. Such competition would preclude the spending of adequate funds to prevent environmental pollution, since this would add tremendously to the cost of the product—unless all other companies would also conform to such antipollution policies. But in a free enterprise economy such policies are not likely to be self-imposed by businessmen. Third, the basic response of the free enterprise system to our economic problems is that we must have greater economic growth or an increase in gross national product. But such growth many ecologists look upon with great alarm, for it can have devastating long-range effects upon our environment. Many of the products of uncontrolled growth are based on artificial needs and actually detract from, rather than contribute to, the quality of our lives. A stationary economy, some economists and ecologists suggest, may well be best for the quality of man's environment and of his life in the long run. Higher GNP does not automatically result in an increase in social well-being, and it should not be used as a measuring rod for assessing economic welfare. This becomes clear when one realizes that the GNP

> aggregates the dollar value of all goods and services produced—the cigarettes as well as the medical treatment of lung cancer, the petroleum from offshore wells as well as the detergents required to clean up after oil spills, the electrical energy produced and the medical and cleaning bills resulting from the air-pollution fuel used for generating the electricity. The GNP allows no deduction for negative production, such as lives lost from unsafe cars or environmental destruction

perpetrated by telephone, electric and gas utilities, lumber companies, and speculative builders.[30]

To many persons, of course, this kind of talk is not only blasphemy but subversive. This is especially true when it is extended in the direction of additional controls over corporate capitalism. (Some ecologists and economists go further and challenge whether corporate capitalism can accommodate a stationary state and still retain its major features.)[31] The fact of the matter is that the ecological attitude forces one to reconsider a host of values which have been held dear in the past, and it forces one to reconsider the appropriateness of the social and economic systems which embodied and implemented those values. Given the crisis of our environment, there must be certain fundamental changes in attitudes toward nature, man's use of nature, and man himself. Such changes in attitudes undoubtedly will have far-reaching implications for the institutions of private property and private enterprise and the values embodied in these institutions. Given that crisis we can no longer look upon water and air as free commodities to be exploited at will. Nor can the private ownership of land be seen as a lease to use that land in any way which conforms merely to the personal desires of the owner. In other words, the environmental crisis is forcing us to challenge what had in the past been taken to be certain basic rights of man or at least to restrict those rights. And it is forcing us to challenge institutions which embodied those rights.

Much has been said in recent months about the conflict between these kinds of rights, and the possible conflict between them is itself a topic for an extensive paper. Depending upon how property rights are formulated, the substantive content of those rights, it seems plain to me, can directly conflict with what we characterize as human rights. In fact our moral and legal history demonstrate exactly that kind of conflict. There was a time in the recent past when property rights embodied the right to hold human beings in slavery. This has now been rejected, almost universally. Under nearly any interpretation of the substantive content of human rights, slavery is incompatible with those rights.

30. See Melville J. Ulmer, "More Than Marxist," *New Republic*, 26 December 1970, p. 14.
31. See Murdock and Connell, "All about Ecology," p. 63.

The analogous question about rights which is now being raised by the data uncovered by the ecologist and by the gradual advancement of the ecological attitude is whether the notion of property rights should be even further restricted to preclude the destruction and pollution of our environmental resources upon which the welfare and the very lives of all of us and of future generations depend. Should our social and legal system embrace property rights or other rights which permit the kind of environmental exploitation which operates to the detriment of the majority of mankind? I do not think so. The fact that a certain right exists in a social or legal system does not mean that it ought to exist. I would not go so far as to suggest that all rights are merely rule-utilitarian devices to be adopted or discarded whenever it can be shown that the best consequences thereby follow.[32] But if a right or set of rights systematically violates the public welfare, this is prima facie evidence that it ought not to exist. And this certainly seems to be the case with the exercise of certain property rights today.

In response to this problem, there is today at least talk of "a new economy of resources," one in which new considerations and values play an important role along with property rights and the interplay of market forces. Economist Nathaniel Wollman argues that "the economic past of 'optimizing' resource use consists of bringing into an appropriate relationship the ordering of preferences for various experiences and the costs of acquiring those experiences. Preferences reflect physiological-psychological responses to experience or anticipated experience, individually or collectively revealed, and are accepted as data by the economist. A broad range of noneconomic investigations is called for to supply the necessary information."[33]

Note that Wollman says that noneconomic investigations are called for. In other words the price system does not adequately account for a number of value factors which should be included in

32. Some rights, I would argue, are inalienable, and are not based merely on a contract (implicit or explicit) or merely upon the norm of maximizing good consequences. (See David Braybrooke's *Three Tests for Democracy: Personal Rights, Human Welfare, Collective Preference* (New York: Random House, 1968), which holds such a rule-utilitarian theory of rights, and my "Human Rights and Human Dignity," for a rebuttal.)

33. Nathaniel Wollman, "The New Economics of Resources," *Daedalus* 96, pt. 2, (Fall 1967): 1100.

an assessment. "It does not account for benefits or costs that are enjoyed or suffered by people who were not parties to the transaction."[34] In a system which emphasizes simply the interplay of market forces as a criterion, these factors (such as sights, smells and other aesthetic factors, justice, and human rights—factors which are important to the well-being of humans) are not even considered. Since they have no direct monetary value, the market places no value whatsoever on them. Can we assume, then, that purely economic or market evaluations provide us with data which will permit us to maximize welfare, if the very process of evaluation and the normative criteria employed exclude a host of values and considerations upon which human welfare depend? The answer to this question is plain. We cannot make this assumption. We cannot rely merely upon the interplay of market forces or upon the sovereignty of the consumer. The concept of human welfare and consequently the notion of maximizing that welfare requires a much broader perspective than the norms offered by the traditional economic perspective. A great many things have value and use which have no economic value and use. Consequently we must broaden our evaluational perspective to include the entire range of values which are essential not only to the welfare of man but also to the welfare of other living things and to the environment which sustains all of life. And this must include a reassessment of rights.

ETHICS AND TECHNOLOGY

I have been discussing the relationship of ecology to ethics and to a theory of rights. Up to this point I have not specifically discussed the relation of technology to ethics, although it is plain that technology and its development is responsible for most of our pollution problems. This topic deserves separate treatment, but I do want to briefly relate it to the thesis of this work.

It is well known that new technology sometimes complicates our ethical lives and our ethical decisions. Whether the invention is the wheel or a contraceptive pill, new technology always opens up new possibilities for human relationships and for society, for

34. Ibid.

good and ill. The pill, for example, is revolutionizing sexual morality, for its use can preclude many of the bad consequences normally attendant upon premarital intercourse. *Some* of the strongest arguments against premarital sex have been shot down by this bit of technology (though certainly not all of them). The fact that the use of the pill can prevent unwanted pregnancy does not make premarital sexual intercourse morally right, nor does it make it wrong. The pill is morally neutral, but its existence does change in part the moral base of the decision to engage in premarital sex. In the same way, technology at least in principle can be neutral—neither necessarily good nor bad in its impact on other aspects of the environment. Unfortunately, much of it is bad—very bad. But technology can be meshed with an ecological attitude to the benefit of man and his environment.

I am not suggesting that the answer to technology which has bad environmental effects is necessarily more technology. We tend too readily to assume that new technological developments will always solve man's problems. But this is simply not the case. One technological innovation often seems to breed a half-dozen additional ones which themselves create more environmental problems. We certainly do not solve pollution problems, for example, by changing from power plants fueled by coal to power plants fueled by nuclear energy, if radioactive waste from the latter is worse than pollution from the former. Perhaps part of the answer to pollution problems is less technology. There is surely no real hope of returning to nature (whatever that means) or of stopping *all* technological and scientific development, as some advocate. Even if it could be done, this would be too extreme a move. The answer is not to stop technology, but to guide it toward proper ends, and to set up standards of antipollution to which all technological devices must conform. Technology has been and can be used to destroy and pollute an environment, but it can also be used to save and beautify it. What is called for is purposeful environmental engineering, and this engineering calls for a mass of information about our environment, about the needs of persons, and about basic norms and values which are acceptable to civilized men. It also calls for priorities on goals and for compromises where there are competing and conflicting values and objectives.

Human rights and their fulfillment should constitute at least some of those basic norms, and technology can be used to implement those rights and the public welfare.

CONCLUSION

It has not been my objective in this essay to enumerate the massive environmental problems which confront us today or to suggest specific answers to them. Rather I have been concerned to explore the implications of ecology and ecological data for ethics in general, for our traditional values, and for a theory of rights in particular. Let me now summarize my basic conclusions: (1) We need a transvaluation of values in regard to attitudes toward nature and the environment. This is not to say that the ecological attitude requires brand new moral principles. The old standbys of justice and the public good are quite satisfactory. But the ecological attitude does require fundamental changes in attitudes toward the environment and a more sophisticated and careful assessment of actions and their effects on the environment than has been done in the past. (2) Although it is essential that the ecological attitude be universally adopted, we must be wary in extending ecological concepts such as stability, equilibrium, or homeostasis into the realm of ethics—at least without proper qualifications. (3) There are objective, cross-culturally accepted norms available for the moral assessment of the impact of actions and policies of action on the environment. (4) There are clear implications of ecological data for a theory of rights and sound grounds for arguing that access to a livable environment is a human right. (5) There are also sound grounds for arguing that this right should become a legal right. (6) Furthermore, although the right to a livable environment may conflict with the right to private property, it is possible to formulate these rights so that they are consistent with one another. (7) However, endorsement of the right to a livable environment as a human and legal right would require new economic theory, one which includes values presently excluded by private business and the mere interplay of market forces. This will require new controls on corporate capitalism or new rules concerning the use of environmental resources within which the private enterprise system is to operate.

The Rights of Animals
and Unborn Generations

JOEL FEINBERG

EVERY PHILOSOPHICAL PAPER must begin with an unproved assumption. Mine is the assumption that there will still be a world
five hundred years from now, and that it will contain human
beings who are very much like us. We have it within our power
now, clearly, to affect the lives of these creatures for better or
worse by contributing to the conservation or corruption of the
environment in which they must live. I shall assume furthermore
that it is psychologically possible for us to care about our remote
descendants, that many of us in fact do care, and indeed that we
ought to care. My main concern then will be to show that it makes
sense to speak of the rights of unborn generations against us, and
that given the moral judgment that we ought to conserve our
environmental inheritance for them, and its grounds, we might
well say that future generations *do* have rights correlative to our
present duties toward them. Protecting our environment now is
also a matter of elementary prudence, and insofar as we do it for
the next generation already here in the persons of our children,
it is a matter of love. But from the perspective of our remote descendants it is basically a matter of justice, of respect for their
rights. My main concern here will be to examine the concept of a
right to better understand how that can be.

THE PROBLEM

To have a right is to have a claim[1] *to* something and *against*
someone, the recognition of which is called for by legal rules or,
in the case of moral rights, by the principles of an enlightened

1. I shall leave the concept of a claim unanalyzed here, but for a detailed
discussion, see my "The Nature and Value of Rights," *Journal of Value In-
quiry* 4 (Winter 1971): 263–277.

conscience. In the familiar cases of rights, the claimant is a competent adult human being, and the claimee is an officeholder in an institution or else a private individual, in either case, another competent adult human being. Normal adult human beings, then, are obviously the sorts of beings of whom rights can meaningfully be predicated. Everyone would agree to that, even extreme misanthropes who deny that anyone in fact has rights. On the other hand, it is absurd to say that rocks can have rights, not because rocks are morally inferior things unworthy of rights (that statement makes no sense either), but because rocks belong to a category of entities of whom rights cannot be meaningfully predicated. That is not to say that there are no circumstances in which we ought to treat rocks carefully, but only that the rocks themselves cannot validly claim good treatment from us. In between the clear cases of rocks and normal human beings, however, is a spectrum of less obvious cases, including some bewildering borderline ones. Is it meaningful or conceptually possible to ascribe rights to our dead ancestors? to individual animals? to whole species of animals? to plants? to idiots and madmen? to fetuses? to generations yet unborn? Until we know how to settle these puzzling cases, we cannot claim fully to grasp the concept of a right, or to know the shape of its logical boundaries.

One way to approach these riddles is to turn one's attention first to the most familiar and unproblematic instances of rights, note their most salient characteristics, and then compare the borderline cases with them, measuring as closely as possible the points of similarity and difference. In the end, the way we classify the borderline cases may depend on whether we are more impressed with the similarities or the differences between them and the cases in which we have the most confidence.

It will be useful to consider the problem of individual animals first because their case is the one that has already been debated with the most thoroughness by philosophers so that the dialectic of claim and rejoinder has now unfolded to the point where disputants can get to the end game quickly and isolate the crucial point at issue. When we understand precisely what *is* at issue in the debate over animal rights, I think we will have the key to the solution of all the other riddles about rights.

INDIVIDUAL ANIMALS

Almost all modern writers agree that we ought to be kind to animals, but that is quite another thing from holding that animals can claim kind treatment from us as their due. Statutes making cruelty to animals a crime are now very common, and these, of course, impose legal duties on people not to mistreat animals; but that still leaves open the question whether the animals, as beneficiaries of those duties, possess rights correlative to them. We may very well have duties *regarding* animals that are not at the same time duties *to* animals, just as we may have duties regarding rocks, or buildings, or lawns, that are not duties *to* the rocks, buildings, or lawns. Some legal writers have taken the still more extreme position that animals themselves are not even the directly intended beneficiaries of statutes prohibiting cruelty to animals. During the nineteenth century, for example, it was commonly said that such statutes were designed to protect human beings by preventing the growth of cruel habits that could later threaten human beings with harm too. Prof. Louis B. Schwartz finds the rationale of the cruelty-to-animals prohibition in its protection of animal lovers from affronts to their sensibilities. "It is not the mistreated dog who is the ultimate object of concern," he writes. "Our concern is for the feelings of other human beings, a large proportion of whom, although accustomed to the slaughter of animals for food, readily identify themselves with a tortured dog or horse and respond with great sensitivity to its sufferings."[2] This seems to me to be factitious. How much more natural it is to say with John Chipman Gray that the true purpose of cruelty-to-animals statutes is "to preserve the dumb brutes from suffering."[3] The very people whose sensibilities are invoked in the alternative explanation, a group that no doubt now includes most of us, are precisely those who would insist that the protection belongs primarily to the animals themselves, not merely to their own tender feelings. Indeed, it would be difficult even to account for the existence of such

2. Louis B. Schwartz, "Morals, Offenses and the Model Penal Code," *Columbia Law Review* 63 (1963): 673.
3. John Chipman Gray, *The Nature and Sources of the Law*, 2d ed. (Boston: Beacon Press, 1963), p. 43.

feelings in the absence of a belief that the animals deserve the protection in their own right and for their own sakes.

Even if we allow, as I think we must, that animals are the intended direct beneficiaries of legislation forbidding cruelty to animals, it does not follow directly that animals have legal rights, and Gray himself, for one,[4] refused to draw this further inference. Animals cannot have rights, he thought, for the same reason they cannot have duties, namely, that they are not genuine "moral agents." Now, it is relatively easy to see why animals cannot have duties, and this matter is largely beyond controversy. Animals cannot be "reasoned with" or instructed in their responsibilities; they are inflexible and unadaptable to future contingencies; they are subject to fits of instinctive passion which they are incapable of repressing or controlling, postponing or sublimating. Hence, they cannot enter into contractual agreements, or make promises; they cannot be trusted; and they cannot (except within very narrow limits and for purposes of conditioning) be blamed for what would be called "moral failures" in a human being. They are therefore incapable of being moral subjects, of acting rightly or wrongly in the moral sense, of having, discharging, or breeching duties and obligations.

But what is there about the intellectual incompetence of animals (which admittedly disqualifies them for duties) that makes them logically unsuitable for rights? The most common reply to this question is that animals are incapable of *claiming* rights on their own. They cannot make motion, on their own, to courts to have their claims recognized or enforced; they cannot initiate, on their own, any kind of legal proceedings; nor are they capable of even understanding when their rights are being violated, of distinguishing harm from wrongful injury, and responding with indignation and an outraged sense of justice instead of mere anger or fear.

No one can deny any of these allegations, but to the claim that they are the grounds for disqualification of rights of animals, philosophers on the other side of this controversy have made con-

4. And W. D. Ross for another. See *The Right and the Good* (Oxford: Clarendon Press, 1930), app. 1, pp. 48–56.

vincing rejoinders. It is simply not true, says W. D. Lamont,[5] that the ability to understand what a right is and the ability to set legal machinery in motion by one's own initiative are necessary for the possession of rights. If that were the case, then neither human idiots nor wee babies would have any legal rights at all. Yet it is manifest that both of these classes of intellectual incompetents have legal rights recognized and easily enforced by the courts. Children and idiots start legal proceedings, not on their own direct initiative, but rather through the actions of proxies or attorneys who are empowered to speak in their names. If there is no conceptual absurdity in this situation, why should there be in the case where a proxy makes a claim on behalf of an animal? People commonly enough make wills leaving money to trustees for the care of animals. Is it not natural to speak of the animal's right to his inheritance in cases of this kind? If a trustee embezzles money from the animal's account,[6] and a proxy speaking in the dumb brute's behalf presses the animal's claim, can he not be described as asserting the animal's *rights?* More exactly, the animal itself claims its rights through the vicarious actions of a human proxy speaking in its name and in its behalf. There appears to be no reason why we should require the animal to understand what is going on (so the argument concludes) as a condition for regarding it as a possessor of rights.

Some writers protest at this point that the legal relation between a principal and an agent cannot hold between animals and human beings. Between humans, the relation of agency can take two very different forms, depending upon the degree of discretion granted to the agent, and there is a continuum of combinations between the extremes. On the one hand, there is the agent who is the mere "mouthpiece" of his principal. He is a "tool" in much the same sense as is a typewriter or telephone; he simply transmits the instructions of his principal. Human beings could hardly be the agents or representatives of animals in this sense, since the dumb brutes could no more use human "tools" than mechanical ones.

5. W. D. Lamont, *Principles of Moral Judgment* (Oxford: Clarendon Press, 1946), pp. 83–85.

6. Cf. H. J. McCloskey, "Rights," *Philosophical Quarterly* 15 (1965): 121, 124.

On the other hand, an agent may be some sort of expert hired to exercise his professional judgment on behalf of, and in the name of, the principal. He may be given, within some limited area of expertise, complete independence to act as he deems best, binding his principal to all the beneficial or detrimental consequences. This is the role played by trustees, lawyers, and ghost-writers. This type of representation requires that the agent have great skill, but makes little or no demand upon the principal, who may leave everything to the judgment of his agent. Hence, there appears, at first, to be no reason why an animal cannot be a totally passive principal in this second kind of agency relationship.

There are still some important dissimilarities, however. In the typical instance of representation by an agent, even of the second, highly discretionary kind, the agent is hired by a principal who enters into an agreement or contract with him; the principal tells his agent that within certain carefully specified boundaries "You may speak for me," subject always to the principal's approval, his right to give new directions, or to cancel the whole arrangement. No dog or cat could possibly do any of those things. Moreover, if it is the assigned task of the agent to defend the principal's rights, the principal may often decide to release his claimee, or to waive his own rights, and instruct his agent accordingly. Again, no mute cow or horse can do that. But although the possibility of hiring, agreeing, contracting, approving, directing, canceling, releasing, waiving, and instructing is present in the typical (all-human) case of agency representation, there appears to be no reason of a logical or conceptual kind why that *must* be so, and indeed there are some special examples involving human principals where it is not in fact so. I have in mind legal rules, for example, that require that a defendant be represented at his trial by an attorney, and impose a state-appointed attorney upon reluctant defendants, or upon those tried *in absentia*, whether they like it or not. Moreover, small children and mentally deficient and deranged adults are commonly represented by trustees and attorneys, even though they are incapable of granting their own consent to the representation, or of entering into contracts, of giving directions, or waiving their rights. It may be that it is unwise to permit agents to represent principals without the latters' knowledge or consent. If so, then no one should ever be permitted to speak for an animal, at least

in a legally binding way. But that is quite another thing than saying that such representation is logically incoherent or conceptually
incongruous—the contention that is at issue.

H. J. McCloskey,[7] I believe, accepts the argument up to this
point, but he presents a new and different reason for denying that
animals can have legal rights. The ability to make claims, whether
directly or through a representative, he implies, is essential to the
possession of rights. Animals obviously cannot press their claims
on their own, and so if they have rights, these rights must be as-
sertable by agents. Animals, however, cannot be represented,
McCloskey contends, and not for any of the reasons already discussed, but rather because representation, in the requisite sense, is
always of interests, and animals (he says) are incapable of having
interests.

Now, there is a very important insight expressed in the require-
ment that a being have interests if he is to be a logically proper
subject of rights. This can be appreciated if we consider just why
it is that mere things cannot have rights. Consider a very precious
"mere thing"—a beautiful natural wilderness, or a complex and
ornamental artifact, like the Taj Mahal. Such things ought to be
cared for, because they would sink into decay if neglected, depriving some human beings, or perhaps even all human beings, of
something of great value. Certain persons may even have as their
own special job the care and protection of these valuable objects
But we are not tempted in these cases to speak of "thing-rights"
correlative to custodial duties, because, try as we might, we cannot
think of mere things as possessing interests of their own. Some
people may have a duty to preserve, maintain, or improve the Taj
Mahal, but they can hardly have a duty to help or hurt it, benefit
or aid it, succor or relieve it. Custodians may protect it for the sake
of a nation's pride and art lovers' fancy; but they don't keep it in
good repair for "its own sake," or for "its own true welfare," or
"well-being." A mere thing, however valuable to others, has no
good of its own. The explanation of that fact, I suspect, consists
in the fact that mere things have no conative life: no conscious
wishes, desires, and hopes; or urges and impulses; or unconscious
drives, aims, and goals; or latent tendencies, direction of growth,
and natural fulfillments. Interests must be compounded somehow

7. Ibid.

out of conations; hence mere things have no interests. *A fortiori*, they have no interests to be protected by legal or moral rules. Without interests a creature can have no "good" of its own, the achievement of which can be its due. Mere things are not loci of value in their own right, but rather their value consists entirely in their being objects of other beings' interests.

So far McCloskey is on solid ground, but one can quarrel with his denial that any animals but humans have interests. I should think that the trustee of funds willed to a dog or cat is more than a mere custodian of the animal he protects. Rather his job is to look out for the interests of the animal and make sure no one denies it its due. The animal itself is the beneficiary of his dutiful services. Many of the higher animals at least have appetites, conative urges, and rudimentary purposes, the integrated satisfaction of which constitutes their welfare or good. We can, of course, with consistency treat animals as mere pests and deny that they have any rights; for most animals, especially those of the lower orders, we have no choice but to do so. But it seems to me, nevertheless, that in general, animals *are* among the sorts of beings of whom rights can meaningfully be predicated and denied.

Now, if a person agrees with the conclusion of the argument thus far, that animals are the sorts of beings that *can* have rights, and further, if he accepts the moral judgment that we ought to be kind to animals, only one further premise is needed to yield the conclusion that some animals do in fact have rights. We must now ask ourselves for whose sake ought we to treat (some) animals with consideration and humaneness? If we conceive our duty to be one of obedience to authority, or to one's own conscience merely, or one of consideration for tender human sensibilities only, then we might still deny that animals have rights, even though we admit that they are the kinds of beings that *can* have rights. But if we hold not only that we ought to treat animals humanely but also that we should do so for the animals' own sake, that such treatment is something we owe animals as their due, something that can be claimed for them, something the withholding of which would be an injustice and a wrong, and not merely a harm, then it follows that we do ascribe rights to animals. I suspect that the moral judgments most of us make about animals do pass these phenomenological tests, so that most of us do believe that animals have rights, but are reluctant to say so because of the conceptual confusions about the notion of a right that I have attempted to dispel above.

Now we can extract from our discussion of animal rights a crucial principle for tentative use in the resolution of the other riddles about the applicability of the concept of a right, namely, that the sorts of beings who *can* have rights are precisely those who have (or can have) interests. I have come to this tentative conclusion for two reasons: (1) because a right holder must be capable of being represented and it is impossible to represent a being that has no interests, and (2) because a right holder must be capable of being a beneficiary in his own person, and a being without interests is a being that is incapable of being harmed or benefitted, having no good or "sake" of its own. Thus, a being without interests has no "behalf" to act in, and no "sake" to act for. My strategy now will be to apply the "interest principle," as we can call it, to the other puzzles about rights, while being prepared to modify it where necessary (but as little as possible), in the hope of separating in a consistent and intuitively satisfactory fashion the beings who can have rights from those which cannot.

VEGETABLES

It is clear that we ought not to mistreat certain plants, and indeed there are rules and regulations imposing duties on persons not to misbehave in respect to certain members of the vegetable kingdom. It is forbidden, for example, to pick wildflowers in the mountainous tundra areas of national parks, or to endanger trees by starting fires in dry forest areas. Members of Congress introduce bills designed, as they say, to "protect" rare redwood trees from commercial pillage. Given this background, it is surprising that no one[8] speaks of plants as having rights. Plants, after all, are not "mere things"; they are vital objects with inherited biological propensities determining their natural growth. Moreover, we do say that certain conditions are "good" or "bad" for plants, thereby suggesting that plants, unlike rocks, are capable of having a "good." (This is a case, however, where "what we say" should not be taken seriously: we also say that certain kinds of paint are good

8. Outside of Samuel Butler's *Erewhon*.

or bad for the internal walls of a house, and this does not commit us to a conception of walls as beings possessed of a good or welfare of their own.) Finally, we are capable of feeling a kind of affection for particular plants, though we rarely personalize them, as we do in the case of animals, by giving them proper names.

Still, all are agreed that plants are not the kinds of beings that can have rights. Plants are never plausibly understood to be the direct intended beneficiaries of rules designed to "protect" them. We wish to keep redwood groves in existence for the sake of human beings who can enjoy their serene beauty, and for the sake of generations of human beings yet unborn. Trees are not the sorts of beings who have their "own sakes," despite the fact that they have biological propensities. Having no conscious wants or goals of their own, trees cannot know satisfaction or frustration, pleasure or pain. Hence, there is no possibility of kind or cruel treatment of trees. In these morally crucial respects, trees differ from the higher species of animals.

Yet trees are not mere things like rocks. They grow and develop according to the laws of their own nature. Aristotle and Aquinas both took trees to have their own "natural ends." Why then do I deny them the status of beings with interests of their own? The reason is that an interest, however the concept is finally to be analyzed, presupposes at least rudimentary cognitive equipment. Interests are compounded out of *desires* and *aims*, both of which presuppose something like *belief*, or cognitive awareness. A desiring creature may want X because he seeks anything that is $\emptyset$, and X appears to be $\emptyset$ to him; or he may be seeking Y, and he believes, or expects, or hopes that X will be a means to Y. If he desires X in order to get Y, this implies that he believes that X will bring Y about, or at least that he has some sort of brute expectation that is a primitive correlate of belief. But what of the desire for $\emptyset$ (or for Y) itself? Perhaps a creature has such a "desire" as an ultimate set, as if he had come into existence all "wound up" to pursue $\emptyset$-ness or Y-ness, and his not to reason why. Such a propensity, I think, would not qualify as a desire. Mere brute longings unmediated by beliefs—longings for one knows not what—might perhaps be a primitive form of consciousness (I don't want to beg that question) but they are altogether different from the sort of thing we mean by "desire," especially when we speak of human beings.

If some such account as the above is correct, we can never have any grounds for attributing a desire or a want to a creature known to be incapable even of rudimentary beliefs; and if desires or wants are the materials interests are made of, mindless creatures have no interests of their own. The law, therefore, cannot have as its intention the protection of their interests, so that "protective legislation" has to be understood as legislation protecting the interests human beings may have in them.

Plant life might nevertheless be thought at first to constitute a hard case for the interest principle for two reasons. In the first place, plants no less than animals are said to have needs of their own. To be sure, we can speak even of mere things as having needs too, but such talk misleads no one into thinking of the need as belonging, in the final analysis, to the "mere thing" itself. If we were so deceived we would not be thinking of the mere thing as a "mere thing" after all. We say, for example, that John Doe's walls need painting, or that Richard Roe's car needs a washing, but we direct our attitudes of sympathy or reproach (as the case may be) to John and Richard, not to their possessions. It would be otherwise, if we observed that some child is in need of a good meal. Our sympathy and concern in that case would be directed at the child himself as the true possessor of the need in question.

The needs of plants might well seem closer to the needs of animals than to the pseudoneeds of mere things. An owner may need a plant (say, for its commercial value or as a potential meal), but the plant itself, it might appear, needs nutrition or cultivation. Our confusion about this matter may stem from language. It is a commonplace that the word *need* is ambiguous. To say that A needs X may be to say either: (1) X is necessary to the achievement of one of A's goals, or to the performance of one of its functions, or (2) X is good for A; its lack would harm A or be injurious or detrimental to him (or it). The first sort of need-statement is value-neutral, implying no comment on the value of the goal or function in question; whereas the second kind of statement about needs commits its maker to a value judgment about what is good or bad for A in the long run, that is, about what is in A's interests.

A being must have interests, therefore, to have needs in the second sense, but any kind of thing, vegetable or mineral, could have needs in the first sense. An automobile needs gas and oil to function, but it is no tragedy for it if it runs out—an empty tank does not hinder or retard its interests. Similarly, to say that a tree needs sunshine and water is to say that without them it cannot grow and survive; but unless the growth and survival of trees are matters of human concern, affecting human interests, practical or aesthetic, the needs of trees alone will not be the basis of any claim of what is "due" them in their own right. Plants may need things in order to discharge their functions, but their functions are assigned by human interests, not their own.

The second source of confusion derives from the fact that we commonly speak of plants as thriving and flourishing, or withering and languishing. One might be tempted to think of these states either as themselves consequences of the possession of interests so that even creatures without wants or beliefs can be said to have interests, or else as grounds independent of the possession of interests for the making of intelligible claims of rights. In either case, plants would be thought of as conceivable possessors of rights after all.

Consider what it means to speak of something as "flourishing." The verb *to flourish* apparently was applied originally and literally to plants only, and in its original sense it meant simply "to bear flowers: BLOSSOM"; but then by analogical extension of sense it came also to mean "to grow luxuriantly: increase, and enlarge," and then to "THRIVE" (generally), and finally, when extended to human beings, "to be prosperous," or to "increase in wealth, honor, comfort, happiness, or whatever is desirable."[9] Applied to human beings the term is, of course, a fixed metaphor. When a person flourishes, something happens to his interests analogous to what happens to a plant when it flowers, grows, and spreads. A person flourishes when his interests (whatever they may be) are progressing severally and collectively toward their harmonious fulfillment and spawning new interests along the way whose prospects are also good. To flourish is to glory in the advancement of one's interests, in short, to be happy.

Nothing is gained by twisting the botanical metaphor back

9. *Webster's Third New International Dictionary.*

from humans to plants. To speak of thriving human interests as if they were flowers is to speak naturally and well, and to mislead no one. But then to think of the flowers or plants as if they were interests (or the signs of interests) is to bring the metaphor back full circle for no good reason and in the teeth of our actual beliefs. Some of our talk about flourishing plants reveals quite clearly that the interests that thrive when plants flourish are human not "plant interests." For example, we sometimes make a flowering bush flourish by "frustrating" its own primary propensities. We pinch off dead flowers before seeds have formed, thus "encouraging" the plant to make new flowers in an effort to produce more seeds. It is not the plant's own natural propensity (to produce seeds) that is advanced, but rather the gardener's interest in the production of new flowers and the spectator's pleasure in aesthetic form, color, or scent. What we mean in such cases by saying that the plant flourishes is that our interest in the plant, not its own, is thriving. It is not always so clear that that is what we mean, for on other occasions there is a correspondence between our interests and the plant's natural propensities, a coinciding of what we want from nature and nature's own "intention." But the exceptions to this correspondence provide the clue to our real sense in speaking of a plant's good or welfare.[10] And even when there exists such a correspondence, it is often because we have actually remade the plant's nature so that our interests in it will flourish more "naturally" and effectively.

WHOLE SPECIES

The topic of whole species, whether of plants or animals, can be treated in much the same way as that of individual plants. A whole collection, as such, cannot have beliefs, expectations, wants, or desires, and can flourish or languish only in the human interest-

---

10. Sometimes, of course, the correspondence fails because what accords with the plant's natural propensities is not in our interests, rather than the other way round. I must concede that in cases of this kind we speak even of weeds flourishing, but I doubt that we mean to imply that a weed is a thing with a good of its own. Rather, this way of talking is a plain piece of irony, or else an animistic metaphor (thinking of the weeds in the way we think of prospering businessmen). In any case, when weeds thrive, usually no interests, human or otherwise, flourish.

related sense in which individual plants thrive and decay. Individual elephants can have interests, but the species elephant cannot. Even where individual elephants are not granted rights, human beings may have an interest—economic, scientific, or sentimental—in keeping the species from dying out, and *that* interest may be protected in various ways by law. But that is quite another matter from recognizing a right to survival belonging to the species itself. Still, the preservation of a whole species may quite properly seem to be a morally more important matter than the preservation of an individual animal. Individual animals can have rights but it is implausible to ascribe to them a right to life on the human model. Nor do we normally have duties to keep individual animals alive or even to abstain from killing them provided we do it humanely and nonwantonly in the promotion of legitimate human interests. On the other hand, we do have duties to protect threatened species, not duties to the species themselves as such, but rather duties to future human beings, duties derived from our housekeeping role as temporary inhabitants of this planet.

We commonly and very naturally speak of corporate entities, such as institutions, churches, and national states as having rights and duties, and an adequate analysis of the conditions for ownership of rights should account for that fact. A corporate entity, of course, is more than a mere collection of things that have some important traits in common. Unlike a biological species, an institution has a charter, or constitution, or bylaws, with rules defining offices and procedures, and it has human beings whose function it is to administer the rules and apply the procedures. When the institution has a duty to an outsider, there is always some determinant human being whose duty it is to do something for the outsider, and when the state, for example, has a right to collect taxes, there are always certain definite flesh and blood persons who have rights to demand tax money from other citizens. We have no reluctance to use the language of corporate rights and duties because we know that in the last analysis these are rights or duties of individual persons, acting in their "official capacities." And when individuals act in their official roles in accordance with valid empowering rules, their acts are imputable to the organization itself and become "acts of state." Thus, there is no need to posit any individual superperson named by the expression "the State" (or for that matter, "the company," "the club," or "the church.") Nor is there any reason to take the rights of corporate entities to be exceptions to the interest principle. The United States is not a superperson with wants and beliefs of its own, but it is a corporate entity with corporate interests that are, in turn, analyzable into the interests of its numerous flesh and blood members.

DEAD PERSONS

So far we have refined the interest principle but we have not had occasion to modify it. Applied to dead persons, however, it will have to be stretched to near the breaking point if it is to explain how our duty to honor commitments to the dead can be thought to be linked to the rights of the dead against us. The case against ascribing rights to dead men can be made very simply: a dead man is a mere corpse, a piece of decaying organic matter. Mere inanimate things can have no interests, and what is incapable of having interests is incapable of having rights. If, nevertheless, we grant dead men rights against us, we would seem to be treating the interests they had while alive as somehow surviving their deaths. There is the sound of paradox in this way of talking, but it may be the least paradoxical way of describing our moral relations to our predecessors. And if the idea of an interest's surviving its possessor's death is a kind of fiction, it is a fiction that most living men have a real interest in preserving.

Most persons while still alive have certain desires about what is to happen to their bodies, their property, or their reputations after they are dead. For that reason, our legal system has developed procedures to enable persons while still alive to determine whether their bodies will be used for purposes of medical research or organic transplantation, and to whom their wealth (after taxes) is to be transferred. Living men also take out life insurance policies guaranteeing that the accumulated benefits be conferred upon beneficiaries of their own choice. They also make private agreements, both contractual and informal, in which they receive promises that certain things will be done after their deaths in exchange for some present service or consideration. In all these cases promises are made to living persons that their wishes will be honored after they are dead. Like all other valid promises, they impose duties on the promisor and confer correlative rights on the promisee.

How does the situation change after the promisee has died? Surely the duties of the promisor do not suddenly become null and void. If that were the case, and known to be the case, there could be no confidence in promises regarding posthumous arrangements; no one would bother with wills or life insurance companies to pay benefits to survivors, which are, in a sense, only conditional duties before a man dies. They come into existence as categorical demands for immediate action only upon the promisee's death. So the view that death renders them null and void has the truth exactly upside down.

The survival of the promisor's duty after the promisee's death does not prove that the promisee retains a right even after death, for we might prefer to conclude that there is one class of cases where duties to keep promises are not logically correlated with a promisee's right, namely, cases where the promisee has died. Still, a morally sensitive promisor is likely to think of his promised performance not only as a duty (i.e., a morally required action) but also as something owed to the deceased promisee as his due. Honoring such promises is a way of keeping faith with the dead. To be sure, the promisor will not think of his duty as something to be done for the promisee's "good," since the promisee, being dead, has no "good" of his own. We can think of certain of the deceased's interests, however, (including especially those enshrined in wills and protected by contracts and promises) as surviving their owner's death, and constituting claims against us that persist beyond the life of the claimant. Such claims can be represented by proxies just like the claims of animals. This way of speaking, I believe, reflects more accurately than any other an important fact about the human condition: we have an interest while alive that other interests of ours will continue to be recognized and served after we are dead. The whole practice of honoring wills and testaments, and the like, is thus for the sake of the living, just as a particular instance of it may be thought to be for the sake of one who is dead.

Conceptual sense, then, can be made of talk about dead men's rights; but it is still a wide open moral question whether dead men in fact have rights, and if so, what those rights are. In particular, commentators have disagreed over whether a man's interest in his reputation deserves to be protected from defamation even after his death. With only a few prominent exceptions, legal systems punish a libel on a dead man "only when its publication is in truth an attack upon the interests of living persons."[11] A widow or a son may be wounded, or embarrassed, or even injured economically, by a defamatory attack on the memory of their dead husband or father. In Utah defamation of the dead is a misdemeanor, and in Sweden a cause of action in tort. The law rarely presumes, however, that a dead man himself has any interests, representable by proxy, that can be injured by defamation, apparently because of the maxim that what a dead man doesn't know can't hurt him.

This presupposes, however, that the whole point of guarding the reputations even of living men, is to protect them from hurt feelings, or to protect some other interests, for example, economic ones, that do not survive death. A moment's thought, I think, will show that our interests are more complicated than that. If someone spreads a libelous description of me, without my knowledge, among hundreds of persons in a remote part of the country, so that I am, still without my knowledge, an object of general scorn and mockery in that group, I have been injured, even though I never learn what has happened. That is because I have an interest, so I believe, in having a good reputation *simpliciter*, in addition to my interest in avoiding hurt feelings, embarrassment, and economic injury. In the example, I do not know what is being said and believed about me, so my feelings are not hurt; but clearly if I did know, I would be enormously distressed. The distress would be the natural consequence of my belief that an interest other than my interest in avoiding distress had been damaged. How else can I account for the distress? If I had no interest in a good reputation as such, I would respond to news of harm to my reputation with indifference.

While it is true that a dead man cannot have his feelings hurt, it does not follow, therefore, that his claim to be thought of no worse than he deserves cannot survive his death. Almost every living person, I should think, would wish to have this interest

11. William Salmond, *Jurisprudence*, 12th ed., ed. P. J. Fitzgerald (London: Sweet and Maxwell, 1966), p. 304.

protected after his death, at least during the lifetimes of those persons who were his contemporaries. We can hardly expect the law to protect Julius Caesar from defamation in the history books. This might hamper historical research and restrict socially valuable forms of expression. Even interests that survive their owner's death are not immortal. Anyone should be permitted to say anything he wishes about George Washington or Abraham Lincoln, though perhaps not everything is morally permissible. Everyone ought to refrain from malicious lies even about Nero or King Tut, though not so much for those ancients' own sakes as for the sake of those who would now know the truth about the past. We owe it to the brothers Kennedy, however, as their due, not to tell damaging lies about them to those who were once their contemporaries. If the reader would deny that judgment, I can only urge him to ask himself whether he now wishes his own interest in reputation to be respected, along with his interest in determining the distribution of his wealth, after his death.

HUMAN VEGETABLES

Mentally deficient and deranged human beings are hardly ever so handicapped intellectually that they do not compare favorably with even the highest of the lower animals, though they are commonly so incompetent that they cannot be assigned duties or be held responsible for what they do. Since animals can have rights, then, it follows that human idiots and madmen can too. It would make good sense, for example, to ascribe to them a right to be cured whenever effective therapy is available at reasonable cost, and even those incurables who have been consigned to a sanatorium for permanent "warehousing" can claim (through a proxy) their right to decent treatment.

Human beings suffering extreme cases of mental illness, however, may be so utterly disoriented or insensitive as to compare quite unfavorably with the brightest cats and dogs. Those suffering from catatonic schizophrenia may be barely distinguishable in respect to those traits presupposed by the possession of interests from the lowliest vegetables. So long as we regard these patients as potentially curable, we may think of them as human beings with interests in their own restoration and treat them as possessors of rights. We may think of the patient as a genuine human person inside the vegetable casing struggling to get out, just as in the old fairy tales a pumpkin could be thought of as a beautiful maiden under a magic spell waiting only the proper words to be restored to her true self. Perhaps it is reasonable never to lose hope that a patient can be cured, and therefore to regard him always as a person "under a spell" with a permanent interest in his own recovery that is entitled to recognition and protection.

What if, nevertheless, we think of the catatonic schizophrenic and the vegetating patient with irreversible brain damage as absolutely incurable? Can we think of them at the same time as possessed of interests and rights too, or is this combination of traits a conceptual impossibility? Shocking as it may at first seem, I am driven unavoidably to the latter view. If redwood trees and rosebushes cannot have rights, neither can incorrigible human vegetables.[12] The trustees who are designated to administer funds for the care of these unfortunates are better understood as mere custodians than as representatives of their interests since these patients no longer have interests. It does not follow that they should not be kept alive as long as possible: that is an open moral question not foreclosed by conceptual analysis. Even if we have duties to keep human vegetables alive, however, they cannot be duties *to* them. We may be obliged to keep them alive to protect the sensibilities of others, or to foster humanitarian tendencies in ourselves, but we cannot keep them alive for their own good, for they are no longer capable of having a "good" of their own. Without awareness, expectation, belief, desire, aim, and purpose, a being can have no interests; without interests, he cannot be benefited; without the capacity to be a beneficiary, he can have no rights. But there may nevertheless be a dozen other reasons to treat him as if he did.

---

12. Unless, of course, the person in question, before he became a "vegetable," left testamentary directions about what was to be done with his body just in case he should ever become an incurable vegetable. He may have directed either that he be preserved alive as long as possible, or else that he be destroyed, whichever he preferred. There may, of course, be sound reasons of public policy why we should not honor such directions, but if we did promise to give legal effect to such wishes, we would have an example of a man's earlier interest in what is to happen to his body surviving his very competence as a person, in quite the same manner as that in which the express interest of a man now dead may continue to exert a claim on us.

FETUSES

If the interest principle is to permit us to ascribe rights to infants, fetuses, and generations yet unborn, it can only be on the grounds that interests can exert a claim upon us even before their possessors actually come into being, just the reverse of the situation respecting dead men where interests are respected even after their possessors have ceased to be. Newly born infants are surely noisier than mere vegetables, but they are just barely brighter. They come into existence, as Aristotle said, with the capacity to acquire concepts and dispositions, but in the beginning we suppose that their consciousness of the world is a "blooming, buzzing confusion." They do have a capacity, no doubt from the very beginning, to feel pain, and this alone may be sufficient ground for ascribing both an interest and a right to them. Apart from that, however, during the first few hours of their lives, at least, they may well lack even the rudimentary intellectual equipment necessary to the possession of interests. Of course, this induces no moral reservations whatever in adults. Children grow and mature almost visibly in the first few months so that those future interests that are so rapidly emerging from the unformed chaos of their earliest days seem unquestionably to be the basis of their present rights. Thus, we say of a newborn infant that he has a right now to live and grow into his adulthood, even though he lacks the conceptual equipment at this very moment to have this or any other desire. A new infant, in short, lacks the traits necessary for the possession of interests, but he has the capacity to acquire those traits, and his inherited potentialities are moving quickly toward actualization even as we watch him. Those proxies who make claims in behalf of infants, then, are more than mere custodians: they are (or can be) genuine representatives of the child's emerging interests, which may need protection even now if they are to be allowed to come into existence at all.

The same principle may be extended to "unborn persons." After all, the situation of fetuses one day before birth is not strikingly different from that a few hours after birth. The rights our law confers on the unborn child, both proprietary and personal, are for the most part, placeholders or reservations for the rights he shall inherit when he becomes a full-fledged interested being. The law protects a potential interest in these cases before it has even grown into actuality, as a garden fence protects newly seeded flower beds long before blooming flowers have emerged from them. The unborn child's present right to property, for example, is a legal protection offered now to his future interest, contingent upon his birth, and instantly voidable if he dies before birth. As Coke put it: "The law in many cases hath consideration of him in respect of the apparent expectation of his birth";[13] but this is quite another thing than recognizing a right actually to be born. Assuming that the child will be born, the law seems to say, various interests that he will come to have after birth must be protected from damage that they can incur even before birth. Thus prenatal injuries of a negligently inflicted kind can give the newly born child a right to sue for damages which he can exercise through a proxy-attorney and in his own name any time *after* he is born.

There are numerous other places, however, where our law seems to imply an unconditional right to be born, and surprisingly no one seems ever to have found that idea conceptually absurd. One interesting example comes from an article given the following headline by the *New York Times:* "Unborn Child's Right Upheld Over Religion."[14] A hospital patient in her eighth month of pregnancy refused to take a blood transfusion even though warned by her physician that "she might die at any minute and take the life of her child as well." The ground of her refusal was that blood transfusions are repugnant to the principles of her religion (Jehovah's Witnesses). The Supreme Court of New Jersey expressed uncertainty over the constitutional question of whether a non-pregnant adult might refuse on religious grounds a blood transfusion pronounced necessary to her own survival, but the court

13. As quoted by Salmond, *Jurisprudence*, p. 303. Simply as a matter of policy the potentiality of some future interests may be so remote as to make them seem unworthy of present support. A testator may leave property to his unborn child, for example, but not to his unborn grandchildren. To say of the potential person presently in his mother's womb that he owns property now is to say that certain property must be held for him until he is "real" or "mature" enough to possess it. "Yet the law is careful lest property should be too long withdrawn in this way from the uses of living men in favor of generations yet to come; and various restrictive rules have been established to this end. No testator could now direct his fortune to be accumulated for a hundred years and then distributed among his descendants"—Salmond, ibid.

14. *New York Times*, 17 June 1966, p. 1.

nevertheless ordered the patient in the present case to receive the transfusion on the grounds that "the unborn child is entitled to the law's protection."

It is important to reemphasize here that the questions of whether fetuses do or ought to have rights are substantive questions of law and morals open to argument and decision. The prior question of whether fetuses are the kind of beings that can have rights, however, is a conceptual, not a moral, question, amenable only to what is called "logical analysis," and irrelevant to moral judgment. The correct answer to the conceptual question, I believe, is that unborn children are among the sorts of beings of whom possession of rights can meaningfully be predicated, even though they are (temporarily) incapable of having interests, because their future interests can be protected now, and it does make sense to protect a potential interest even before it has grown into actuality. The interest principle, however, makes perplexing, at best, talk of a noncontingent fetal right to be born; for fetuses, lacking actual wants and beliefs, have no actual interest in being born, and it is difficult to think of any other reason for ascribing any rights to them other than on the assumption that they will in fact be born.[15]

FUTURE GENERATIONS

We have it in our power now to make the world a much less pleasant place for our descendants than the world we inherited from our ancestors. We can continue to proliferate in ever greater numbers, using up fertile soil at an even greater rate, dumping our wastes into rivers, lakes, and oceans, cutting down our forests, and polluting the atmosphere with noxious gases. All thoughtful people agree that we ought not to do these things. Most would say that we have a duty not to do these things, meaning not merely that conservation is morally required (as opposed to merely desirable) but also that it is something due our descendants, something to be done for their sakes. Surely we owe it to future genera-

15. In an essay entitled "Is There a Right to be Born?" I defend a negative answer to the question posed, but I allow that under certain very special conditions, there can be a "right *not* to be born." See *Abortion*, ed. J. Feinberg (Belmont, Calif.: Wadsworth, 1973).

tions to pass on a world that is not a used up garbage heap. Our remote descendants are not yet present to claim a livable world as their right, but there are plenty of proxies to speak now in their behalf. These spokesmen, far from being mere custodians, are genuine representatives of future interests.

Why then deny that the human beings of the future have rights which can be claimed against us now in their behalf? Some are inclined to deny them present rights out of a fear of falling into obscure metaphysics, by granting rights to remote and unidentifiable beings who are not yet even in existence. Our unborn great-great-grandchildren are in some sense "potential" persons, but they are far more remotely potential, it may seem, than fetuses. This, however, is not the real difficulty. Unborn generations are more remotely potential than fetuses in one sense, but not in another. A much greater period of time with a far greater number of causally necessary and important events must pass before their potentiality can be actualized, it is true; but our collective posterity is just as certain to come into existence "in the normal course of events" as is any given fetus now in its mother's womb. In that sense the existence of the distant human future is no more remotely potential than that of a particular child already on its way.

The real difficulty is not that we doubt whether our descendants will ever be actual, but rather that we don't know who they will be. It is not their temporal remoteness that troubles us so much as their indeterminacy—their present facelessness and namelessness. Five centuries from now men and women will be living where we live now. Any given one of them will have an interest in living space, fertile soil, fresh air, and the like, but that arbitrarily selected one has no other qualities we can presently envision very clearly. We don't even know who his parents, grandparents, or great-grandparents are, or even whether he is related to us. Still, whoever these human beings may turn out to be, and whatever they might reasonably be expected to be like, they will have interests that we can affect, for better or worse, right now. That much we can and do know about them. The identity of the owners of these interests is now necessarily obscure, but the fact of their interest-ownership is crystal clear, and that is all that is necessary to certify the coherence of present talk about their rights. We can tell, sometimes, that shadowy forms in the spatial distance belong to human beings, though we know not who or how many they are; and this imposes a duty on us not to throw bombs, for example, in their direction. In like manner, the vagueness of the human future does not weaken its claim on us in light of the nearly certain knowledge that it will, after all, be human.

Doubts about the existence of a right to be born transfer neatly to the question of a similar right to come into existence ascribed to future generations. The rights that future generations certainly have against us are contingent rights: the interests they are sure to have when they come into being (assuming of course that they will come into being) cry out for protection from invasions that can take place now. Yet there are no actual interests, presently existent, that future generations, presently nonexistent, have now. Hence, there is no actual interest that they have in simply coming into being, and I am at a loss to think of any other reason for claiming that they have a right to come into existence (though there may well be such a reason). Suppose then that all human beings at a given time voluntarily form a compact never again to produce children, thus leading within a few decades to the end of our species. This of course is a wildly improbable hypothetical example but a rather crucial one for the position I have been tentatively considering. And we can imagine, say, that the whole world is converted to a strange ascetic religion which absolutely requires sexual abstinence for everyone. Would this arrangement violate the rights of anyone? No one can complain on behalf of presently nonexistent future generations that their future interests which give them a contingent right of protection have been violated since they will never come into existence to be wronged. My inclination then is to conclude that the suicide of our species would be deplorable, lamentable, and a deeply moving tragedy, but that it would violate no one's rights. Indeed if, contrary to fact, all human beings could ever agree to such a thing, that very agreement would be a symptom of our species' biological unsuitability for survival anyway.

CONCLUSION

For several centuries now human beings have run roughshod over the lands of our planet, just as if the animals who do live there and the generations of humans who will live there had no claims on them whatever. Philosophers have not helped matters by arguing that animals and future generations are not the kinds of beings who can have rights now, that they don't presently qualify for membership, even "auxiliary membership," in our moral community. I have tried in this essay to dispel the conceptual confusions that make such conclusions possible. To acknowledge their rights is the very least we can do for members of endangered species (including our own). But that is something.

APPENDIX

The Paradoxes of Potentiality

Having conceded that rights can belong to beings in virtue of their merely potential interests, we find ourselves on a slippery slope; for it may seem at first sight that anything at all can have potential interests, or much more generally, that anything at all can be potentially almost anything else at all! Dehydrated orange powder is potentially orange juice, since if we add water to it, it will be orange juice. More remotely, however, it is also potentially lemonade, since it will become lemonade if we add a large quantity of lemon juice, sugar, and water. It is also a potentially poisonous brew (add water and arsenic), a potential orange cake (add flour, etc., and bake), a potential orange-colored building block (add cement and harden), and so on, *ad infinitum*. Similarly a two-celled embryo, too small to be seen by the unaided eye, is a potential human being; and so is an unfertilized ovum; and so is even an "uncapacitated" spermatozoan. Add the proper nutrition to an implanted embryo (under certain other necessary conditions) and it becomes a fetus and then a child. Looked at another way, however, the implanted embryo has been combined (under the same conditions) with the nutritive elements, which themselves are converted into a growing fetus and child. Is it then just as proper to say that food is a "potential child" as that an embryo is a potential child? If so, then what isn't a "potential child?" (Organic elements in the air and soil are "potentially food," and hence potentially people!)

Clearly, some sort of line will have to be drawn between direct or proximate potentialities and indirect or remote ones; and however we draw this line, there will be borderline cases whose classification will seem uncertain or even arbitrary. Even though any *X* can become a *Y* provided only that it is combined with the necessary additional elements, *a*, *b*, *c*, *d*, and so forth, we cannot say of any given *X* that it is a "potential *Y*" unless certain further—rather strict—conditions are met. (Otherwise the concept of potentiality, being universally and promiscuously applicable, will have no utility.) A number of possible criteria of proximate potentiality suggest themselves. The first is the criterion of causal importance. Orange powder is not properly called a potential building block because of those elements needed to transform it into a building block, the cement (as opposed to any of the qualities of the orange powder) is the causally crucial one. Similarly, any pauper might (misleadingly) be called a "potential millionaire" in the sense that all that need be added to any man to transform him into a millionaire is a great amount of money. The absolutely crucial element in the change, of course, is no quality of the man himself but rather the million dollars "added" to him.

What is causally "important" depends upon our purposes and interests and is therefore to some degree a relativistic matter. If we seek a standard, in turn, of "importance," we may posit such a criterion, for example, as that of the ease or difficulty (to some persons or other) of providing those missing elements which, when combined with the thing at hand, convert it into something else. It does seem quite natural, for example, to say that the orange powder is potentially orange juice, and that is because the missing element is merely common tap water, a substance conveniently near at hand to everyone; whereas it is less plausible to characterize the powder as potential cake since a variety of further elements, and not just one, are required, and some of these are not conveniently near at hand to many. Moreover, the process of combining the missing elements into a cake is rather more complicated than mere "addition." It is less plausible still to call orange powder a potential curbstone for the same kind of reason. The criterion of ease or difficulty of the acquisition and combination of additional elements explains all these variations.

Still another criterion of proximate potentiality closely related to the others is that of degree of deviation required from "the normal course of events." Given the intentions of its producers, distributors, sellers, and consumers, dehydrated orange juice will, in the normal course of events, become orange juice. Similarly, a human embryo securely imbedded in the wall of its mother's uterus will in the normal course of events become a human child. That is to say that if no one deliberately intervenes to prevent it happening, it will, in the vast majority of cases, happen. On the other hand, an unfertilized ovum will not become an embryo unless someone intervenes deliberately to make it happen. Without such intervention in the "normal" course of events, an ovum is a mere bit of protoplasm of very brief life expectancy. If we lived in a world in which virtually every biologically capable human female became pregnant once a year throughout her entire fertile period of life, then we would regard fertilization as something that happens to every ovum in "the natural course of events." Perhaps we would regard every unfertilized ovum, in such a world, as a potential person even possessed of rights corresponding to its future interests. It would perhaps make conceptual if not moral sense in such a world to regard deliberate nonfertilization as a kind of homicide.

It is important to notice, in summary, that words like *important*, *easy*, and *normal* have sense only in relation to human experiences, purposes, and techniques. As the latter change, so will our notions of what is important, difficult, and usual, and so will the concept of potentiality, or our application of it. If our purposes, understanding, and techniques continue to change in indicated directions, we may even one day come to think of inanimate things as possessed of "potential interests." In any case, we can expect the concept of a right to shift its logical boundaries with changes in our practical experience.

The Environmental Results
of Technology

CHARLES HARTSHORNE

MY ASTUTE FORMER COLLEAGUE Charner Perry long ago pointed out that every invention designed to enable us to cope with existing difficulties or dangers introduces new difficulties and new dangers. He was entirely right, and I can think of no exception. With automobiles we can move—and also die—in unprecedented ways. In addition we destroy beautiful forest, prairie, or agricultural land to make surfaces which are useless save for transportation. And we pollute air and water, and this not only directly by the cars, but also by the factories that make them. Any substitutes will do some of these things.

I now announce a truth that some wise men of the last century thought they saw very well: what technology produces is not necessarily an essentially better life for the privileged members of society. Jane Austen's Emma and Mr. Knightley led very good lives indeed. Aristotle lived a life satisfying on a high level. What professor today does much better? Think of the quality of Shakespeare's experience as poet and dramatist, exploring imaginatively the heights and depths of human possibility. Technology does principally two things: First—and this was less clearly seen by our forefathers—technological progress, although it scarcely improves what life at its best affords, does fantastically increase the number of those for whom that best is available. Second, technology allows a great number of people at least a marginal existence.

As Ortega y Gasset points out, technology makes kingly luxuries commonplaces for large numbers of people. True enough, as Ortega also points out, it makes luxuries even beyond the reach of kings of the past, for example, aspirin and radio, similarly commonplace. But these luxuries are not essential to life on a high level. Even printing is not essential for that. Before printing there were scholarship and communication from mind to mind through the generations in both Europe and Asia. There were novels, essays, poems, dramas, letters, all the essentials of culture, but they were available to far fewer readers. Technology multiplies participation in the chief values, far more than the values themselves.

The contrast between the Amerindians and the European settlers illustrates the point very well. The settlers knew that with their culture they could make it possible for many more individuals to live reasonably well in North America than the Indians could with theirs. They thought they also knew that each individual would be living better, but this is debatable. The Indians knew loyalty, democratic self-government, love of spouse and children, sense for the beauties of nature, reverence for the divine, humor, zestful rivalry, poetry, music—in short, the essential human values. But after many thousands of years there were only a million or so Indians in North America.

Technology, besides making it possible for larger numbers to enjoy the goods of life, makes it possible for an additional huge number to live at least marginally, and even marginal living is better than nothing. The will to live may be sustained by minimal satisfactions, but they are still satisfactions. In sum, technology has greatly enlarged three groups of people, those with minimal, mediocre, or optimal modes of living.

There is one group which technology has not enlarged, and that is the nonhuman living creatures on this planet. As humanity expands, most other life-forms diminish. Where dead concrete is now, myriads of living species once flourished; where a few species of grains and a few sorts of animals now grow, thousands of kinds of plants and animals requiring forest, swamp, or wild prairie once enjoyed their lives in their own nonhuman way. There are some exceptions. A few species of plants and animals (probably including rats) are now more numerous than formerly, but on the whole the amount and variety of nonhuman life is being steadily diminished. To take one example, the Humpbacked Whale—a marvelous creature, in some respects closer to man even than the apes, a creature having a well-developed song, and a uniquely complex one at that—is threatened with extinction. Our pesticides are threats to most forms of life—including our own.

At this point we come finally face-to-face with the environmental problem in its current form. For it is now clear that not only does technological man expand at the expense of other forms of life but in principle he faces limits beyond which his own expansion is impossible or self-defeating. Did any philosopher foresee this outcome? In general, philosophers have not been very much given to prophecy, whether pessimistic or optimistic. Thus Aristotle said (seemingly as a *reductio ad absurdum*) that slavery could be abolished only if men acquired machines that operated themselves. That such machines would be invented did not apparently occur to him. The power of human thought to change the world has proved far greater in some respects than philosophers so much as dreamed. Alas, in some other respects the power of thought to change things is still to be demonstrated. After all the philosophy, theology, and science, people continue to act not only from self-interest but also from blind passions, including malice and sadistic pleasure.

We face the question, To what extent is multiplication of the number of persons living, on no matter what cultural level, an objective which should take precedence over the question of maintaining, and if possible elevating, the level? The argument that it is unnatural to take effective steps to limit births is no longer cogent, for modern hygiene has destroyed the nature in question, the nature in which man and other forms of life were in a nearly stable balance, and the waste products of human living could be absorbed by the general environment—that is, by the other creatures making up this part of the solar system. Natural law is a fine thing, but one must know one's nature. The nature the pope seems to know about is gone.

That each additional person adds value to the world I hold to be undeniable. But each person also detracts from the value of the world. This too must not be forgotten. He competes with others, at the very least for air, food, water, and absorption of his waste products. The common query, "Is so and so worth his salt?" expresses sound philosophy. Only it should now run, "Is he worth his air, water, parking space, and opportunity to relieve himself?"

Another ethical question concerns the competition between man and other forms of life. That a person is of more value than a sparrow is acceptable, although some Asiatic religions seem a little unclear about this. But even the religions that want us to spare other animals wherever possible seem to have thought in terms of individuals, not of species. A species through many generations is a vast multitude of individuals. I have yet to hear of a Hindu, Buddhist, or Jain who has worried about the possible extinction of entire species by destruction of their habitats. Yet in my view this is an incomparably more serious offense. An animal lives but a few years at most, and it does not know its mortality as we do. That an animal may later be killed by a hunter, or in a slaughterhouse, is no bar to its enjoyment of life while it is living in a reasonably normal way. And if the slain animal has produced offspring successfully, its mode of enjoyment can go on for centuries or even millennia. But if the habitat is razed or poisoned, then this mode of enjoyment comes to an end. I fail to find any clear ideas about this in historical religions or philosophies.

To risk a man's or woman's life for a subhuman individual is, I believe, unwarranted. But to do so to save an entire species, say of whale, ape, or elephant, would this be unwarranted? I'm not so sure. In the biblical tradition the other animals were said to be there for the sake of man. Still, cruelty to animals was frowned upon, and in Job and in the sayings of Jesus there seems to be a feeling that the nonhuman creatures have their own values, apart from any utility they have for us. "Ye are of more value than many sparrows," but this implies that they too have some value. No form of life should be thought a mere means, a mere utility. All forms are beautiful and good in themselves. Here I agree with Schweitzer against Kant, and I counter Kant's contention that only the rational being has intrinsic value by the following points. First, as Kant admitted, only deity is without qualification "rational" in the sense here relevant; second, as Kant did not admit, all creatures, no matter how little or much rational they are, have only so much value as they contribute, and they all do contribute value to the divine life which alone is, without qualification, "end in itself." All creatures are for the "glory of God." The most decisive difference is not between human and subhuman, though that difference is real and important, but between divine and not divine.

Though the foregoing for me furnishes the meaning of life, it does not tell me how to compare the value of additional masses of human beings with that of preserving the specific variety of non-human nature. That this variety has value for man, as every zoo illustrates, is not the only or perhaps even the essential point. The variety has value for the other animals themselves and for God. But how much value? Here I feel somewhat at a loss.

However, since man himself is threatened by his proliferation and his greed for luxuries which he has ever greater difficulty of disposing of when he is through with them, or the production of which pollutes air and water, and destroys wild nature or agricultural land, the interest some of us feel in the other animals as having intrinsic value points to some extent at least toward the same practical conclusion as our interest in human welfare. This conclusion is that we need to rethink our desire for luxuries, as well as for numerous offspring.

I do not own a car and do ride a bicycle. There are several reasons for this: but one of them is the conviction I acquired long ago that if we really love nature we must be critical of advertisers and friends or neighbors who tell us that the good life means the life of many possessions. I really agree with Asiatics who say that Americans are too materialistic. The charge is often made, maybe tinged with envy and hypocrisy, and also with some ignorance of how we really live in this country, but still, allowing for all such qualifications, I hold that the charge goes home. We care too much about physical possessions and too little about spiritual ones. American mothers are fanatically anxious that their children avoid dirt and possible germs, but how anxious are they that the children will learn by parental example what sound, healthy, happy thoughts are like? Small children learn to love others by finding them lovable; they learn to be happy by sharing in the happiness of those close to them. If infants begin life by experiencing the misery of being unloved and of being surrounded with discontented or malicious people, how will they ever later form healthy emotional habits? The Asiatics know all this; many American parents seem scarcely to have an inkling of it. There is no great mystery in the children of the rich being sometimes unhappy. In early life the greatest possible gift to a child, granted that it is nourished reasonably well, is to feel itself in the midst of love and happiness. What are expensive clothes and toys compared to this?

If the environment is to be spared, some people must give up some things. Material goods are always competitive; the natural environment is a material or physical good. To save it, material sacrifices are necessary. As someone has said, the environmental question is, who is going to do without what?

It is important to realize that all forms of power involve pollution. Electricity seems clean in our houses but the generating plants are not and never will be entirely so. To heat a home by electricity at present produces at least twice as much pollution at the plant as burning oil does at the home.[1] All extravagant uses of current need to be discouraged—for instance, by raising rates for large usage instead of lowering them. (Power ought long ago, as Henry Simons for one suggested, to have been frankly socialized, since it is not free or competitive enterprise).[2] Advertising encouraging extravagant living and wasting paper and other materials needs to be sharply curtailed by law, as Simons also suggested. A beginning has now been made with cigarettes, and liquor is an obvious next step, but there is no reason to stop there. Our entire system of values needs reconsideration, for plainly it is out of tune with present and far more with probable future conditions. The rest of the world knows that there are things wrong with traditional Americanism. It is our obligation to know it even better and to face these problems constructively. To combat pollution, one of the prime problems, some sacrifice is required of us all. We can flatten tin cans and save glass containers, sacrificing time and energy to do it.

"How hardly shall a rich man enter into the kingdom!" I have never felt that preachers did very well with that text. I take it seriously, and I think it has secular as well as religious validity. Also, by world standards, half of our population is, or is trying to be, rich. Some of our youth do well to query this ideal.

At least half the battle of saving the environment is of course slowing down, then stopping, and then perhaps reversing, the population growth. *How?* is what nobody seems to know. But one thing is clearly required: men, and women too, must change some ideas about the roles of women. Technology has reduced the time

1. David R. Inglis, "Nuclear Energy and the Malthusian Dilemma," *Science and Public Affairs* 27, no. 2 (1971): 14–18. Note especially p. 18.
2. Henry Simons, *Economic Policy for a Free Society* (Chicago: University of Chicago Press, 1948).

needed for childbearing as well as the time needed for house-keeping. It has greatly lengthened women's lives. Either they are then (on the average) to spend most of these lives doing little that is socially honored, or they must be given additional and more adequate opportunities in politics, the arts and sciences, professions, businesses. If not, they will continue—as their one significant function—to have more babies than are needed or than they really want. And unwanted children grow up to plague us all.

That women are not fairly treated in academic life is obvious. A recent article by the historian Ann Harris in the September 1970 *Bulletin of the AAUP* is relevant here. She documents "widespread discrimination against women in all strata of higher education." And what an illustration of human weakness it is that though men write most of the academic publications, it has to be women who bother to dig up the facts on this question in a scholarly way. All our boasted objectivity and intellectual discipline do not overcome the partiality of men for their sex. For thousands of years men (e.g., Aristotle) have talked in ways that can be proved to be fallacious about the natural inferiority of women, ignoring the tremendous handicaps that primitive hygiene (hence necessity for numerous births), powerful social customs, and simple male self-ishness have imposed upon women. And the *Bulletin* shows that men are still at it, including academic men.

The qualification "on the average" inserted above is important. All sorts of special cases are to be admitted, including admirably old-fashioned, happy, and good mothers of numerous children. But the average case can no longer be of that kind. We have an unprecedented world on our hands.

The feeling on the part of the young that this age is so new that historical precedents are of little help is partly justified. Education has failed to train for flexibility in meeting new conditions to nearly the needed extent. Even so, in some degree, environmental problems are old. For thousands of years men have been burning or otherwise destroying forests, often leaving eroded barren hills; there has for ages been some effort in many parts of the world to limit childbearing. However, the discovery of North and South America reinstated the illusion of an unlimited nature which in the civilized Old World has been partly overcome. There was thus a dangerous regression, and our still not-quite-banished idea of the normal family, like our idea of a "square meal," arises partly from now irrelevant pioneer experiences.

We must rethink our design for living. We still do not have a responsible attitude toward childbearing or toward the values and disvalues of luxurious living. Even our idolatry of cleanliness, putting everything in plastic and the like, is grossly exaggerated and one more cause of pollution. Our extravagant use of water to have the same sort of lawns and gardens everywhere can, I imagine, hardly survive the coming water shortages. We need to value native plants more and cultivated ones less. We need to have more sense for the glory of nature as she is, or was, apart from man. Yet it may be that wild nature on this planet is almost completely doomed. The population figures strongly suggest this, together with the rising demand for luxuries around the world. It may be so. But for some of us this is not a happy thought. For me a natural forest is inexpressibly beautiful. No parks, plantations, or gardens compare with it, for the forest shelters thousands, in the tropics tens of thousands, of wondrously varied kinds of creatures, leaping, climbing, flying, singing—every one a unique, harmonious pattern of life.

A sticky aspect of the environmental crisis is that although every increase in production tends to increase pollution and destruction of nature the present level of production leaves half of mankind poorly supplied. And there is no sign of populations ceasing to increase in the next decade or two—quite the contrary. Consequently, unless production increases a good deal, either the rich and moderately well-to-do will make severe material sacrifices, or the underprivileged will be even worse off than they are now. Zero population growth in the near future is not to be expected, zero economic growth will be cruelty to millions unless the richer half of mankind become a lot more like saints—or genuine Christians or Buddhists—than seems probable. No matter how one calculates, the environmental prospects are grim. Centuries of loose thinking, flabby optimism, stupid or hypocritical social ethics or lack of ethics are catching up with us.

I understand, I think, why many blacks today find talk about saving the environment leaving them cold. They sometimes react to proposals to limit childbearing as attempts of the "master race" to reduce their relative power. I have some sympathy for the feeling that only through numbers can the dark-skinned receive the attention they must have from American society as a whole. For the lingering folly of racism I see no long-run remedy apart from intermarriage, against which (as the ultimate desideratum) the arguments seem to me weak. As for the environment, how shall anyone brought up in a ghetto know or feel the beauty of wild nature? In the old days in the southeastern states, many Negroes living away from cities were good, if unscientific, naturalists. They were all their lives acquainted with nature's variety. But the main mass of blacks are now far removed from anything of the sort. So this, too, is a tragic difficulty of our time. Wild nature as represented by a ghetto rat, or a few house sparrows or pigeons, is hardly calculated to win affection.

Perhaps, however, black men as well as white should be willing to save their women from the bitter tragedy of unwanted child-bearing. So much is bare justice to one's own nearest and dearest. The arrogance of men toward women is not racist: it is traditionally human.

The young are right; it is a new day. Indeed it is newer than they think. What is new about cigarette smoking, or the use of hashish? Asia has tried the latter for centuries. Smoking is another form of pollution, and, as Dick Gregory points out, the tobacco industry is a pillar of the establishment. We need to lessen our dependence upon inessential material goods, not increase it. We need to recover the old sense of the sages that to be a functioning human being in a functioning universe is already and in itself a glorious thing. What more we demand is a subject for calm deliberation, the results of which will show our wisdom or folly.

Our young utopians perhaps miss something which most of their elders also lack. This is an understanding of the root source of evil in existence. Plato, Hobbes, and Kant had some understanding of the political dangers inherent in our natures, which, as Ortega says, means chiefly our histories. But neither "nature" nor "history" quite hits the target. I hold that, until recently, not a single major philosopher saw clearly the root cause of destruction, suffering, and evil. That cause is the cosmic principle of freedom. In spite of all the causal order in the world there is, as many legends attest, an element of chaos at the heart of reality. What is that chaos? Quite simply, it is multiple freedom, self-determination of the many impinging upon the self-determination of each one. As Plato said, more truly than he quite knew, the soul is self-moved and the secret of all motion. No god and no human arrangements could guarantee perfect order or harmony, either in human life or in the world anywhere. For each being must, at each moment, make *its* decision for that moment. Not simply human beings, but all beings must do this. Those who know Peirce or Whitehead should grasp my meaning. By good luck the multiple decisions of men and other creatures will in many cases fit together harmoniously; by bad luck they will in many cases result in conflict. The higher the level of being, the greater the freedom, and hence the greater the possible ills implied by "bad luck." It is, I am convinced, mere superstition—indeed, mere confusion—to suppose that even ideal or divine power could conceivably eliminate all aspects of risk from the freedom which inheres in concrete actuality. On humble levels, actuality implies trifling forms of freedom, hence trifling forms of risk; on high levels, nontrifling forms. Man is the freest creature, hence the most dangerous to himself and others. This is what it is to be human. The great opportunities of the human kind or degree of freedom mean also great risks. Technology magnifies both opportunities and risks because it magnifies the scope of the choices inherent in freedom.

Man, Nature,
and the History of Philosophy

WALTER H. O'BRIANT

MY STUDY of the history of Western philosophy indicates that there have been two quite different ways of viewing the relation between man and nature. These views have not always been explicitly formulated or even clearly distinguished from one another. Indeed, over the history of Western thought it has been usual for these two views to be so intertwined with one another that it becomes quite difficult for the interpreter of the thought of a given man or movement to delineate these views and determine their importance in relation to other views.

In this essay I propose to define these two views with particular attention to our Western tradition and the role which they have played in shaping our current notions about man and his relation to nature. I intend to show that a part of our inability to deal conceptually with what has come to be called "the crisis of the environment" is due to a failure to be clear and consistent about what we believe to be the nature of man and to understand fully the implications of these beliefs.

TWO VIEWS OF MAN AND NATURE

I propose to designate these two views as "man apart from nature" and "man a part of nature." The view that man is apart from nature is a corollary of the belief that man is a unique creature. Historically, those who hold this belief have maintained that man possesses a faculty which sets him apart from all other creatures. Man alone has a soul—or, more precisely, a rational soul. Thus, man is different *in kind* from everything else in creation. It is noteworthy here that this characterization has been made in relation to the notions of creature, Creator, and creation, for in our religious tradition particularly the basis for man's uniqueness has been found in his relation to his Creator. The most important feature of this relation is that man was made in the image of God.

Now whatever specific interpretation we put upon this notion of *imago Dei*, it seems clear that it is an attempt to assert a degree of similarity between whatever it is which makes man man and his Creator. "We were made in His likeness." For some interpreters this has been a matter even of physical resemblance such as we find in Michelangelo's depiction of God giving life to Adam. For others, man is godlike in his ability to reason. But in any case man occupies a very special place. He belongs, as it were, to two worlds. He is a creature, and so is a natural man. Yet he is also made in the image of his Creator, and so is a supernatural man, one who in some way transcends the bounds of nature.

This special relation to his Creator means also that man has a special relation to the other creatures. He has dominion over them, signified in our tradition by the claim that Adam gave the names to all the other creatures. According to this view the other creatures were put here by the Creator for man's use and enjoyment.

This ambiguous status of man has been most often expressed in our tradition by the claim that, when a man dies, his body returns to the earth from whence it came and his soul—or some part of it—returns to the Creator. Thus the natural man, corruptible man, is mortal, but supernatural man, incorruptible man, is immortal. Such a view constitutes a rather explicit dualism: a man consists of two elements, a body and a soul, neither of which is reducible to or derivative from the other. The body is material; the soul, immaterial. And this dualistic view involves an additional ambiguity by leaving unsettled the answer to the question, What is man?

On the one hand, it has been maintained that man is composed of both a soul and a body, each having characteristics which fit it to be a *human* soul or a *human* body, as the case may be. But neither a body alone nor a soul alone can constitute a human being on this view. A man cannot be a disembodied spirit or an unensouled body. In the dance of life, on this view it "takes two to tango." Anything less must be either superhuman or subhuman. Man then is a natural being.

In contrast, there has been at least an equally strong tendency in our tradition to hold that man is essentially a soul, his body being an unnecessary and even obstructing adjunct. What makes us what we are is our soul. Our body is at best an earthen vessel which the soul occupies during its brief sojourn in this world; at worst the body is a tomb for the soul, preventing it from achieving its highest potentialities by weighing it down with the bodily appetites for the things of this world. Only when it is freed from bondage can the soul soar to the heights of which it is capable. Our life so far as this world is concerned must be one of constant vigilance lest we succumb to the demands of the body and thereby condemn our soul. Man then is a supernatural being who finds himself for the moment in a natural world—a world which cannot be his home.

Consequently, the question What is man? is open to two quite different answers. The proponents of the first view would say that man is composed of a soul and a body somehow constituting a unity, while the proponents of the second view would hold that man is a soul and his body plays no significant role in making him what he is. Strange as it might seem in view of our quite pronounced tendency to establish personal identity on the basis of bodily characteristics such as one's height, manner of speaking, or fingerprints, the latter view—that the body is nonessential—seems to have been the dominant one in our tradition.

This brings us to the second view—the view that man is a part of nature. For the advocates of this view, man is not unique—at least not in the sense that he possesses some special faculty which no other living thing possesses. Rather man is seen as one animal among many other animals from whom he differs, not in kind, but only in degree. His distinctiveness is not a matter of possessing a soul or some special kind of a soul which no other animal possesses; it is a matter of his possessing certain abilities to a higher—or lower—degree. Thus, for example, man is distinguished from the other animals, not by mere rationality, but by the degree to which he is capable of exercising this reason.

On this view, it is no "slap in the face" to say of a man that he behaves like an animal; he *is* an animal, and it would be paradoxical were he to behave in some other way. Man is an animal among his fellow animals. He has not been given "dominion" over them except in the sense in which any living thing possessing some relatively high-order function has "dominion" over other living things which possess that function to a lesser degree. More-over, like all the other animals, man is mortal. He has his day—"three score years and ten"—and then perishes just as they do; though perhaps generally not so violently or miserably. "Ashes to ashes; dust to dust." His mortality is mitigated only to the ex-tent that he may be remembered by his fellows or may have played some significant role in shaping the welfare of his society or species.

This view is quite clearly monistic. Man consists fundamentally of one sort of stuff, body, and this is the stuff out of which every-thing else in the universe is made. The world of nature is all there is. There is no supernatural realm, no soul which survives the death of the body, no spiritual Creator presiding over the natural world. Man is his own last, best hope. What is man? The pro-ponents of this view would answer: one of the animals, distinctive in certain respects, but not unique. We find this view quite ex-plicitly in the zoologist Desmond Morris's contention that were we to compare man with the so-called apes the only truly distinc-tive human feature would be the relative absence of body hair. Hence the title of Morris's book *The Naked Ape.* Quite literally, we and the apes are brothers under the skin, and in Morris's view it is our failure to recognize fully our animality which has cost us so dearly both individually and socially.

RELIGION AND SCIENCE

Despite the relatively clear distinctions between these two views of man and nature which have been outlined above and the quite different sets of corollary views which belong to each, we have tried in our tradition to hold on rather firmly to both of them without making the major revisions which would be requisite for resolving conflicts between these views. Moreover, each of these views has become so firmly embedded in a major element of our tradition that for many an attempt at revision would require either a major recasting of that element or its total rejection—perhaps without being able to find a suitable substitute. The two elements involved here are religion and science.

Our religious tradition—the Judeo-Christian tradition—has been dominated by the first view, the view that man is apart from nature. It has rather consistently held that this world is not our home, that our primary business—indeed our only business—is the salvation of our immortal souls, and that our animal nature is vile and contemptible. There is then a distinctively "otherworldly" character to this element of our tradition.

Our scientific tradition, in contrast, has—at least in more recent times—embraced the view that man is a part of nature and that comprehending the character and function of man is not fundamentally different from that of the proverbial white rat, the amoeba, or the rings of Saturn. Man's make-up may be a bit more complicated and his behavior relatively sophisticated, but he is at bottom explicable in the same terms as everything else in nature. The exclusion from the scientific element of such notions as soul and Creator has been reinforced by the scientist's insistence that all legitimate claims must be open to empirical investigation; it must be possible to see or taste or in some other way sense them. The consequence of this view has been to give a decidedly "this worldly" emphasis to the scientific element. The claims for a supernatural realm are either regarded as not legitimate concerns of the scientist or, more likely, dismissed as without foundation in fact.

We should not then be amiss to call our first view the religious view and our second the scientific view.

CARTESIANISM

These tendencies are clearly reflected in the thought of René Descartes whose philosophical views so dominated the early modern period that they became the commonsense views of succeeding centuries and have persisted relatively unchanged into our own time. With a brashness and optimism typical of the early modern period Descartes took upon himself the task of reconstituting philosophy so as to ensure a firm foundation upon which to erect a sound superstructure. A metaphysics firmly rooted in its method would yield as its fruit a sound mechanics, medicine, and morals. And the method which Descartes pursued was that of doubt—the refusal to give his assent to any proposition which seemed open to the least questioning.

The initial result of this method in Descartes's hands was to lay open the possibility of doubting the existence of the external world and even that of a benevolent God. The only thing of which

Descartes could be initially assured was his own existence. His certainty of this lay in the dictum *cogito, ergo sum.* Consequently, in attempting to answer the question Who am I? Descartes characterized himself solely as "a thing which thinks."

Thus this phase of his thought embodies two of the most fundamental aspects of the religious view: (1) I am essentially a soul (since only a soul can think), and (2) the external world—which is material—is less real than my self—which is spiritual. There is also a third element, a radical subjectivism, which, though not prominent in our religious tradition until modern times, has come to assume an increasingly conspicuous role, particularly in the development of what is usually called "Protestantism"—a view which now ranges far beyond its original religious context.

But Descartes was not content to stop at this point and the second phase of his thought resulted in a radically different position. Descartes was also convinced that what was so persistently and strongly impressed upon his senses, namely, the corporeal world, could not be ultimately unreal or illusory even though he might be misled in a particular instance about the character of some detail of that world. The influence of atomism and his own investigations in analytics and physics disposed him to believe that the method for understanding this world must be essentially mathematical.

In this second phase of his thought Descartes is much more the scientific man. He is committed to (1) the reality of an independent external world (corporeal substance in particular) and (2) its comprehension by quantization. The opposing commitments which shaped Descartes's philosophy have continued to pull at us. In particular this vacillation has prevented us from adopting a consistent, adequate attitude toward ourselves and our world.

To the extent that we are religious men we have been willing to divide the furniture of the universe into two kinds: the furniture of earth, which is material, inert, and corruptible, and the furniture of heaven, which is spiritual, living, and incorruptible. Man as a creature little lower than the angels has a foot in both worlds; he is lord of the earth, and it is intended for his use as he makes his journey through this land of cares and temptations on his way to his true home.

This careless attitude toward his environment has been rein-forced by what we may call a frontier attitude—the notion that whenever our surroundings are depleted of the elements needed for our mode of life there will always be virgin territory open for our expropriation and exploitation. Just as we tend to see our-selves as exempt from the fate which has befallen other creatures in the course of natural history, so we also regard our present and future as free from the consequences of our past misbehavior. Our God shall save us from our sins, and we shall ultimately be trans-ported to glory to live forever in comfort and ease.

To the extent that we are scientific men we have come to view everything as ultimately reducible to atoms in motion, the inter-actions of which are describable in terms of physical laws which hold with absolute certainty. Any uncertainty is due to our ob-servational or experimental limitations, not to some indeterminacy about behavior at the atomic and subatomic level. Man like every-thing else is explicable in terms of collocations of atoms following inexorable laws. There is no place here for such notions as "soul." Witness how psychology—literally, the study of the *psyche*—has turned increasingly toward the view that its proper sphere of study is overt human and animal behavior. The treatment of mental ill-ness is now seen largely as a matter of manipulating the processes of a physical organ, the brain, and its associated systems by drugs or surgery, not the attempt to treat some nonphysical entity called "the mind." One of the most basic assumptions of contemporary science is that results obtained from experiments with the so-called lower animals are applicable to man also with the only changes in applicability being those of degree, not of kind.

As religious men, we have thought of the universe as embodying certain moral and aesthetic values and as being ultimately friendly and supportive toward man because we live under the watchful and loving care of a fatherly Creator. But as scientific men, we see the universe as morally and aesthetically neutral. Whatever morality and beauty we see is solely in the eye of the beholder. Likewise, the universe is neither supportive nor hostile as far as man is concerned; it is simply neutral. Whatever Creator there might once have been has now retired from the scene, and the universe is left to operate according to its laws. Miracles simply do not happen.

Thus we find ourselves with two world views which involve quite different sorts of beliefs and commitments. The religious man is ill at ease with the scientific man, and the result is that most of us suffer from a split personality. We have attempted to reduce the conflict between these different views by compartmentalizing them. For some six days of the week we are scientific men, accepting with little misgiving the presuppositions and ramifications of the atomic theory and indeed rejoicing in the devices which the resulting technology has made available for our comfort and amusement. On perhaps one day of the week we are religious again, reaffirming our belief in the existence of a spiritual realm where we find forgiveness for our iniquity and healing for our diseases. But of course the compartmentalization does not work. The rationale for some of our actions is based upon one view; the rationale for others upon the second view. And the disconsonance of these actions soon becomes obvious.

The crisis of the environment is just one aspect of the vastly more pervasive crisis of our culture—our failure to deal promptly, efficiently, and effectively with this dichotomy. Our religious views allowed us to be comfortable in raping and pillaging this earthly abode because we saw ourselves as not ultimately a part of this world and we failed to recognize that having dominion over the earth involved exercising responsible stewardship over it, while our scientific theories again and again proclaimed that we were part of nature and that whatever affected any aspect of nature would ultimately have its effect upon us. We are beginning to see —though only dimly—the terrible price which we shall have to pay for our past negligence. The injury inflicted upon our fellow creatures, especially those yet unborn, is beyond estimation. But we have not yet begun to deal constructively with the more fundamental problem of developing a consistent, adequate, and unambiguous view of man's relation to nature. Until we have done so, our attempts at resolution will be like the shuffling of the pieces of a puzzle which do not fit.

PROPHETS WITHOUT HONOR

The historian of philosophy can only imagine how different our attitude toward nature and ourselves would have been had we taken seriously the criticisms leveled against Descartes by two of his immediate successors, Benedict Spinoza and Gottfried Leibniz. It has been said that alien philosophies are rarely refuted, just ignored. Whether generally true, Spinoza and Leibniz are surely two instances in relation to Cartesianism.

Spinoza attacked Descartes on one of the most central doctrines of his system, namely, the definition of substance as that which can exist in and through itself. It follows from this definition, Spinoza argued, that there can be only one substance, one genuine individual, in the entire universe—or, more precisely, one genuine individual who *is* the entire universe. Unlike Descartes, Spinoza did not assign to individual human beings existence which was relatively independent of and superior to the world at large. Instead Spinoza asserted that everything is ultimately a manifestation of the one, infinite, eternal substance. Nature and God are not two distinct entities; they are the same thing seen from different viewpoints.

Spinoza then was led to a monistic view. Moreover, since everything is the manifestation of an absolute unity the universe is fully intelligible. There is no surd, no arational aspect. Nor is there any miraculous intervention or disruption of the order of things.

Thus, from Descartes's own assumption about the nature of substance, Spinoza formulated a position which not only denied the conclusions to which Descartes thought he was properly led but also embodied two main tenets of the scientific view: (1) Man is not fundamentally different from the other aspects of nature, and (2) nature is all there is. But Spinoza's system also had a fatal dualism. Spinoza held that thought and extension are two of an infinite number of attributes under which the one substance manifests itself. One and the same thing might be viewed under the attribute of thought and under the attribute of extension, but the attributes had coordinate status and thus constituted a parallelism. Thus despite the postulation of one substance the Spinozistic universe remained bifurcated.

It was Leibniz who came closest to locating and removing the presupposition which made both Cartesianism and Spinozism untenable. Leibniz very much admired the world view of the ancient Greek atomists, particularly their emphasis upon qualitative differences as resolvable into quantitative differences, but he found their characterization of the atoms lacking. He saw that so long as we begin with a concept of matter as passive and characterized essentially by occupying space then we shall not be able to bridge the gulf between matter and mind and we shall not be able to extricate ourselves from all the problems inherent in appeals to a purely mechanical model for explaining the universe. Leibniz comprehended more clearly than his two predecessors how the life history of a given thing is inextricably intertwined with that of everything else. I am what I am and the universe is what it is because of the relation which holds between us. Were I or the universe different then the other would be significantly altered.

Leibniz refused to admit any such ultimate distinctions as living versus nonliving, man versus animals. He insisted that any such seeming differences in kind are resolvable into differences in degree. The world of nature stretches along a continuum from the lowest to the highest form with imperceptible shadings from one form to its neighboring forms. Consequently, Leibniz argued, the universe must be viewed as an organism, not a machine. The seemingly inert and lifeless aspect of the universe is simply the limiting case at the lower end of the continuum. The universe is fundamentally alive.

Such a view has seemed to many scientists to smack of "vitalism" —a view which they find abhorrent, and they have tended to summarily reject it. Yet it is remarkable how close Spinoza and especially Leibniz came to espousing on philosophical grounds much of what ecologists and conservationists are now urging on scientific grounds.

PHILOSOPHY, RELIGION, AND ECOLOGY

Our understanding of our world and of ourselves has been perverted by a faulty religion and philosophy which we have used as instruments to pay homage to our ego, and in tragic terms we are paying the price for our sin of pride. But a healthy religious and philosophical outlook can do much to help us remove the critical state in which we find ourselves and our environment. We need a Weltanschauung—a view of the whole—to guide us in establishing our priorities for action. Science and technology can give us the means, but religion and philosophy must delineate the ends.

The abandonment of atomistic individualism and the adoption of an holistic approach must be a task not only for the ecologist, but also for the philosopher, the theologian, indeed for everyman. This will not be accomplished easily or quickly, for the concepts which we need to overhaul are among the most fundamental of our culture. They are embedded in our laws and customs, our traditions and our institutions. We shall have to write a new ethic and reorient ourselves to a quite different world. A difficult task? Yes, and an imperative one. We really have no choice if man and nature are to thrive.

The Environmental Crisis
and the Quality of Life

NICHOLAS RESCHER

INTRODUCTION

MOST OF US tend to think of the environmental crisis as resulting from "too much"—too much pollution, wastage, pesticide, and so forth. But from the economists' angle the problem is one of *scarcity:* too little clean air, pure water, recreationally usable land, safe fruit. The answer traditional among welfare economists to problems of scarcity is based singlemindedly on the leading idea of *production.* But alas the things which the environmental crisis leaves in too short supply—fresh air, clean rivers, unpolluted beaches, and the like are not things to which the standard, traditional concept of the production of goods and services—or anything like it—will be applicable. The project of *producing* another planet earth to live on after we have used this one up is unfortunately unfeasible.

For reasons such as this various economists—Kenneth Boulding most prominent among them—have urged a broadening of economic horizons and redeployment of concern. Economics is to deal not just narrowly with the production and consumption of goods and services but broadly with the maintenance of a quality of life. Such a reorientation of welfare economics has profound consequences. It once again renders relevant to economics the traditional concerns of the philosopher with matters of norms and values, of ideology and the rational structure of social appraisal.

It is from this philosophical vantage point—not ignoring the concerns of the economist and sociologist and social psychologist but seeking to transcend the bounds of their disciplinary bailiwicks —that I should like to consider the impact of the environmental crisis.

Most of the discussions of the environmental crisis in which I have been a participant or witness are basically exercises in social uplift. The lesson is driven home that if only we are good and behave ourselves everything will come out just fine. To adopt more stringent legislation of control, to subject grasping enterprise to social pressure, to adopt better social values and attitudes, to espouse the program and ideology of planned parenthood or women's lib, to hand the control of affairs over to those who are younger and purer of heart . . . so runs the gamut of remedies which their respective advocates would have us adopt and which, once adopted, will—so we are told—put everything to rights. Throughout this stance there runs the fundamentally activistic optimism of the American experience: virtue will be rewarded; and by the end of the sixth reel, the good guys will be riding off into the glorious sunset.

My aim is to dash some cold water on all this. I want to propose the deeply pessimistic suggestion that, crudely speaking, the environment has had it and that we simply cannot "go home again" to "the good old days" of environmental purity. We all know of the futile laments caused by the demise of the feudal order by such thinkers as Thomas More or the ruralistic yearnings voiced by the romantics in the early days of the Industrial Revolution. Historical retrospect may well cast the present spate of hand-wringing over environmental deterioration as an essentially analogous—rightminded but utterly futile—penchant for the easier, simpler ways of bygone days. Actually even to think of the problem as an environmental crisis is tendentious. Crises are by definition transitory phenomena: they point toward a moment of decision for life or death, not toward a stable condition of things. The very terminology indicates an unwillingness to face the prospect of a serious environmental degradation as a permanent reality, an ongoing "fact of life."

To take this view goes deep against the grain, and I have little hope of persuading many people of its correctness. I certainly do not like it myself. But perhaps it could be granted—at least for the sake of discussion—that the view might be correct. Granting this hypothesis, let us explore its implications.

First let me be clearer about the hypothesis itself. I am not saying that environmental activism is futile—that man cannot by dint of energy and effort manage to clean up this or that environmental mess. What I am saying is that we may simply be unable to solve the environmental crisis as a whole: that once this or that form of noxiousness is expelled from one door some other equally bad version comes in by another. My hypothesis in short is that the environmental crisis may well be incurable. It just may be something that we cannot solve but have to learn to live with.

This hypothesis is surely not altogether unrealistic and fanciful. Basically the environmental mess is a product of the conspiration of three forces: (1) high population densities, (2) high levels of personal consumption, and (3) a messy technology of production. Can one even realistically expect that any of these can really be eliminated? Not the population crunch surely. As the character remarked in a recent "Peanuts" cartoon: "Everybody says there are too many of us, but nobody wants to leave." So much for population. Moreover, lots of people everywhere in the world are clamoring for affluence and a place on the high-consumption bandwagon, and pitifully few are jumping off. Nor save in certain high-publicity areas are we likely to get an environmentally benign technology of production and consumption. (I am not enough of a bookworm to start eating the evening newspaper no matter how palatable they make it.) All in all, it takes much doing to persuade oneself that the day of environmental pleasantness is somehow just around the corner. Thus the hypothesis I am asking you to indulge in is not altogether visionary.

I should like in my discussion to dwell on some of the items of the American social ideology that will have to go by the boards if my pessimistic hypothesis is anything like correct.

The first and foremost of these is something I shall characterize under the rubric of the escalation of expectations.

THE ESCALATION OF EXPECTATIONS

The concept of social *progress* is deeply, almost irremovably, impressed on the American consciousness. And this is so not just in the remote past but very much in our own day. Take just the most recent period since World War II. Consider the marked signs of progress:

(1) The increase of life expectancy (at birth) from sixty-three years in 1940 to seventy years in 1965.

(2) The rise of per capita personal income from $1,810 in 1950 to $2,542 in 1965 (in constant [1958] dollars).

(3) The increase in education represented by a rise in school enrollments from 44 percent of the five-to-thirty-four-year-old group in 1950 to 60 percent in 1965.

(4) The growth of social welfare expenditures from $88 per capita in 1945 to $360 per capita in 1965 (in constant [1958] dollars).

Taken together, these statistics bring into focus the steady and significant improvement in the provisions for individual comfort and social welfare that has taken place in the United States since World War II. If the progress-oriented thesis that increased physical well-being brings increased happiness were correct, one would certainly expect Americans to be substantially happier today than ever before. This expectation is not realized. In fact, the available evidence all points the reverse way.

A substantial body of questionnaire data has been completed over the recent years that makes possible a survey of trends in the self-evaluated happiness of Americans. Operating with increasing sophistication, various polling organizations have made their rounds taking massive samples of representative Americans as to their degree of happiness: whether "very happy" or "fairly happy" or "not happy"—or the usual "don't know." The principal findings are set out in schematic form in table 1.[1] There is doubtless *some* looseness in the comparison of these data collected by somewhat different procedures by different organizations.[2] But a relatively clear and meaningful picture emerges all the same: around a fairly stable middle group of "fairly happy" people (some 50 plus or minus 5 percent of the respondents) there is, during the 1941–1965 period an erosion of the sizable initial "very happy" group resulting in a near doubling of the category of those who class themselves "not happy." A definite trend emerges: with the

1. In gathering together the questionnaire data on happiness I have been greatly aided by an unpublished report by Drs. Norman C. Dalkey and Ralph J. Lewis of the RAND Corporation.

2. For example, the Gallup people used "fairly happy" for the middle group while NORC and SRC used "pretty happy."

passage of years since World War II Americans on balance perceive themselves to be increasingly less happy.

TABLE I

Self-Classification of Americans in Point of Happiness
(Results of some Questionnaire Studies)

Year and Organization	Very Happy	Fairly Happy	Not Happy	Don't Know	Score
1946 (AIPO)[a]	39%	50%	9%	2%	110[d]
1947	38	57	4	1	125
1949	43	44	12	1	106
1957 (SRC)[b]	35	54	11		102
1963 (NORC)[c]	32	51	16		83
1965 (NORC)[c]	30	53	17		79

a. AIPO = American Institute of Public Opinion, Princeton, New Jersey (Gallup Organization). Data from Hazel Erskine, "The Polls: Some Thoughts about Life and People," *Public Opinion Quarterly* 28, no. 3 (Fall 1964): 517–528.

b. SRC = Survey Research Center, University of Michigan. Data from Gerald Gruin, Joseph Veroff, and Sheila Feld, *Americans View Their Mental Health* (Basic Books: New York, 1960), p. 22.

c. NORC = National Opinion Research Center, University of Chicago. Data from Norman M. Bradburn, *The Structure of Psychological Well-Being* (Chicago: Aldine-Atherton, 1969), chap 3, table 3.1.

d. In the case of the 1946 data, an international comparison is possible:

Country (Organization)	Very Happy	Fairly Happy	Not Happy	No Response	Score
USA (AIPO)	39%	50%	9%	2%	110
Great Britain (BIPO)	38	56	6		120
Canada (CIPO)	32	55	13		93

See Hadley Cantril and Mildred Strunk, *Public Opinion: 1935–1946* (Princeton, N.J.: Princeton University Press, 1951), p. 281.

NOTE: In computing the "score" we set *very happy* = +2, *fairly happy* = +1, *not happy* = −2, and *don't know* = 0.

The evidence considered in table I relates to the subjective impression of the people interviewed. But there are also relevant data of a more objective kind that indicate a failure of Americans to achieve a higher plateau of personal happiness in the wake of substantial progress in the area of social welfare. For one thing the suicide rate per one hundred thousand population per annum has hovered with remarkable stability in the eleven plus or minus one-half region ever since World War II. Moreover, since 1945 a steadily increasing number of Americans are being admitted to mental hospitals, and, on the average, are spending an increasingly long stay there. And statistical indicators of this sort are readily matched by any number of more subjective psychiatric data. Moreover, even political observers, who certainly have their hand on the nation's pulse, have begun to be concerned over our inability to translate augmented personal affluence into increases in happiness. Thus President Nixon in his first State of the Union message said: "Never has a nation seemed to have had more and enjoyed less." And in his recent book *Rich Man, Poor Man*[3] Henry Miller, chief of the Population Division of the Bureau of the Census, observes that: "We seem to be getting richer and richer in the number of things we own and poorer in our ability to enjoy them."

Thus the upshot of a scrutiny of the available evidence, through personal impressions as well as overt indicators, suggests that it would be the very reverse of the truth to claim that America's impressive postwar progress in matters of human welfare has been matched by a corresponding advance in human happiness. How is this startling implication to be accounted for?

The desired account can, it would seem, be given in something like the following terms: an individual's assessment of his happiness is a matter of his personal and idiosyncratic perception of the extent to which the conditions and circumstances of his life meet his needs and aspirations. And here we enter the area of "*felt* sufficiency" and "*felt* insufficiency." A person might meaningfully say: "I realize full well that, by prevailing standards, I have no good reason to be happy and satisfied with my existing circumstances, but all the same I am perfectly happy and quite contented." Or, on the other hand, he may conceivably say, "I know full well that I have every reason for being happy, but all the same I am extremely discontented and dissatisfied."

3. New York: Thomas Y. Crowell, 1971.

In this context one is carried back to the old proportion of the school of Epicurus in Antiquity.[4]

$$\text{Degree of satisfaction} = \frac{\text{attainment}}{\text{expectation}}$$

The man whose personal vision of happiness calls for yachts and polo ponies will be a malcontent in circumstances many of us would regard as idyllic. He who asks but little may be blissful in very humble circumstances. It is all a matter of how high one reaches in terms of one's expectations and aspirations.

On this basis, it becomes possible to provide a readily intelligible account for the on-first-view startling phenomenon of increasing discontent in the present era of improving personal prosperity and increasing public care for private welfare. For what we are facing is an escalation of expectations, a raising of the levels of expectations with corresponding increased aspirations in the demands people make upon the circumstances and conditions of their lives. With respect to the requisites of happiness, we are in the midst of a revolution of rising expectations, a revolution that affects not only the man at the bottom, but operates throughout, to the very top of the heap.

This supposition of an escalation of expectations regarding the quality of life, and correspondingly of aspirations regarding the requisites of happiness, finds striking confirmation in the fact that despite the impressive signs that people think of themselves as less happy than their predecessors of a generation or so ago, they would be quite unwilling to contemplate a return to what we hear

4. One of the few empirical case studies I am acquainted with that revolves about this bit of speculative philosophy regarding the relationship between expectation and (probable) achievement is: Arnold Thomsen: "Expectation in Relation to Achievement and Happiness," *Journal of Abnormal Social Psychology* 38 (1943): 58–73. Other related discussions and further references are given in James G. March and H. Simon, *Organizations* (New York: Wiley, 1958); Richard M. Cyert and James G. March, *A Behavioral Theory of the Firm* (Englewood Cliffs, N.J.: Prentice-Hall, 1963); T. Costello and S. Zalkind, *Psychology in Administration* (Englewood Cliffs, N.J.: Prentice-Hall, 1963); see pt. 2, "Needs, Motives, and Goals." It is worth noting that often one finds "aspiration" in place of "expectation" in the denominator of the basic proposition. The difference is important but subtle. The enterprising person may aspire to more than he expects to realize; the all-out optimist may expect to realize more than what he aspires to.

spoken of (usually cynically) as the good old days. Let us examine this evidence.

The best starting point here is the core conception of the good old days—the widely accepted idea that people were happier in the days of yore.[5] Table 2 presents findings on people's feelings about the past over a period of years.

Uniformly, the result on such questionnaires as shown in table 2 has been to maintain time and again (usually by a ratio of two to one or more) that Americans were happier in the earlier period. Recognizing the real improvements in the circumstances of life as regards health and knowledge, the bulk of representative American respondents see themselves as living in days when there is less peace of mind, more to worry about, and correspondingly a decline in the general level of personal happiness.

In the face of such a widespread consensus that Americans were happier a generation or so ago, it would seemingly follow that people would hanker after the so-called good old days of earlier times. One would expect to find that many or most people would prefer to have lived in this bygone, happier period. So, indeed, it might well appear. But the actual fact is just the reverse of this expectation.

The findings in table 3 are quite typical. Invariably, Americans reject the would-have-lived-then-rather-than-now option by a ratio of better than two to one. What are we to make of this? I think the answer is relatively clear. So emphatic an indication of the unwillingness of people to trade their circumstances for those of what they have themselves judged to be happier times suggests that Americans have come *to require more* of life to achieve a given level of happiness.[6] Their view seems to be: "To be sure, given what little people asked of life in those 'simpler' days, what

5. Of course, judgments of this sort—even about oneself—are notoriously problematic:

> It is hard enough to know whether one is happy or unhappy now, and still harder to compare the relative happiness or unhappiness of different times of one's life; the utmost that can be said is that we are fairly happy so long as we are not distinctly aware of being miserable.—Samuel Butler, *The Way of All Flesh*

6. One is put in mind of the biblical dictum: "He who is sated loathes honey, but to one who is hungry everything bitter is sweet." (Proverbs 27:7)

TABLE 2

The Good Old Days

Question, Organization, Date	*Yes*	*No*	*No Opinion*[a]
Do you think Americans were happier and more contented thirty years ago than they are today? (AIPO, 1939)	61%	23%	16%

Question, Organization, Date	*Happier*	*Not as Happy*	*No Difference*	*No Opinion/ and Other*
Science has made many changes in the way people live today as compared with the way they lived fifty years ago. On the whole, do you think people are happier than they were fifty years ago because of those changes, or not as happy? (Roper/Minnesota, 1955)	36%	47%	15%	3%

Question, Organization, Date	*More Today*	*Less Today*	*No Difference*	*Don't Know/ No Answer*
Thinking of life today compared to back when your parents were about your age—do you think people today generally have more to worry about than back then, less to worry about, or that there's not much difference? (Roper/Minnesota, 1963)	68%	8%	20%	4%

Question, Organization, Date	Better	Worse	No Difference	No Opinion
Do you think the human race is getting better or worse from the standpoint of health? Knowledge? Moral conduct? Faith in religion? Inner happiness? Peace of Mind? (AIPO, 1949)				
Knowledge	82%	7%	7%	4%
Health	73	18	6	3
Faith in Religion	33	42	18	7
Inner Happiness	21	51	18	10
Moral Conduct	21	52	22	6
Peace of Mind	17	62	11	10
Opinion on peace of mind, by education:				
College	16	74	6	4
High School	18	63	11	8
Grade School	17	57	13	13

a. For comparable and supporting data see Hadley Cantril and Mildred Strunk, *Public Opinion: 1935–1946* (Princeton, N.J.: Princeton University Press, 1951), p. 280.

TABLE 3

Return to the Good Old Days

Question, Organization, Date	Yes	No	No Opinion
Do you wish you were living in those days (thirty years ago) rather than now? (AIPO, 1939)	30%	61%	9%
Do you think you would have rather lived during the horse-and-buggy days instead of now? (Roper, 1939)	25	70	5 *Other*
If you had the choice, would you have preferred to live in the "good old days" instead of in the present period? (Roper/Minnesota, 1956)	15	57	29

they had was quite sufficient to render them happy, or at any rate, happier than we are today—we who have more than they. But of course we, with our present expectations, would not be very happy in their shoes." This position makes manifest the phenomenon we have spoken of as an escalation of expectations.[7] This sort of perception of unhappiness has a surprising twist to it. It indicates a deep faith in progress—a progression of steady improvement in the circumstances of life, however little we may actually savor this improvement in terms of increased happiness.

SOME IDEOLOGICAL VICTIMS

Let us now return on the light of these considerations to my initial hypothesis. If in the continued unfolding an ongoing environmental crisis occurs, various conceptions integral to the American social ideology will have to go by the board: in particular the

7. There may, of course, also be an element of dislike of change and fear of the unknown which has us "rather bear those ills we have, than fly to others that we know not of."

conceptions of material progress, of technological omnipotence, and of millenial orientation.

Material Progress. We have cited evidence of the antipathy of Americans to the idea of a "golden age," a time in the past when conditions of life were superior to those of our own day. The concept of the good old days is in fact wholly anathema to us when the terms of reference are material rather than moral. (Americans have usually been prepared to grant that the "founding fathers" were better men than their contemporaries, but they have never been prepared to concede that they were better off.) We have in general had a fervent commitment to the concept of material progress—that everything is getting bigger and better (or almost everything—occasional exceptions may be conceded [trains, restaurant service]).

A parting of the ways with the concept of progress will not come easy to us. It's going to take a lot of doing to accustom us to the idea that things are on balance to get worse or at any rate no better as concerns the quality of life in this nation. (And once we are persuaded of this, there may be vast social and political repercussions in terms of personal frustration and social unrest.) The conception of a deescalation of expectations, of settling for less than we've been accustomed to, is something Americans are not prepared for. We have had little preparatory background for accepting the realization that in some key aspects in the quality of life the best days may be behind us. I myself very much doubt that we are going to take kindly to the idea. The British have made a pretty good show of having to haul down the flag of empire. You will, I hope, forgive me for evincing skepticism about our ability to show equally good grace when the time comes to run down our banner emblazoned with "Standard of Living."

Technological Omnipotence. The conception of get-it-done confidence, virtually of technological omnipotence, runs deep in the American character. We incline to the idea that, as a people, we can do anything we set our mind to. In a frontier nation there was little tendency toward a serious recognition of limits of any sort. The concept of finite resources, the reality of opportunity costs, the necessity for *choice* in the allocation of effort and the inescapable prospect of unpleasant consequences of choices (negative externalities) are newcomers to American thinking. This era of economic awareness and recognition of the realities of cost-benefit analysis is so recent it has hardly trickled down to the popular level.

The course of our historical experience has not really prepared us to face the realities of finiteness and incapacity. We expect government to "handle things"—not only the foreign wars, economic crises, and social disorders of historical experience, but now the environmental crises as well. The idea that our scientific technology and the social technology of our political institutions may be utterly inadequate to the task does not really dawn on us. If and when it finally does, you may be sure that the fur will fly.

Millenial Hankerings. Americans have manifested more millenial hankerings than perhaps any other people since the days when apocalyptic thinking was in fashion. The idea that a solution to our problems lies somehow just around the corner is deeply ingrained in our consciousness. Nobody knows the themes to which people resonate better than politicians. And from Woodrow Wilson's Fourteen Points to Franklin Roosevelt's New Deal to the quality-of-life rhetoric of Lyndon Johnson's campaign the fundamentally millenial nature of our political rhetoric is clear. "Buy our program, accept our policies, and everything in the country will be just about perfect." That is how the politicians talk, and they do so because that is what people yearn to hear. We can accept deprivation now as long as we feel assured that prosperity lies just around the corner. No political campaign is complete without substantial pandering to our millenial yearnings through assurances that if only we put the right set of men in office all our troubles will vanish and we can all live happily ever after. We as a nation have yet to learn the unpleasant lesson that such pie-in-the-sky thinking is a luxury we can no longer afford.

The ideological consequences of the demise of a faith in progress, technological omnipotence, and the millenial orientation will clearly be profound. The result cannot but be a radically altered ideology, a wholly new American outlook. What will this be? All too temptingly it may be a leap to the opposite extreme: to hopelessness, despondency, discouragement—the sense of impotence and *après nous le déluge.* I am afraid that such an era of disillusionment may well be the natural consequence of the presently popular rhetoric of the environmental crisis. And the American people do not have a particularly good record for sensible action in a time of disappointed expectations. Our basic weakness is a rather nonstandard problem of morale: a failure not of nerve but of patience.

Yet such a result—despair and disillusionment—seems to me wholly unwarranted. It is realism not hopelessness that provides the proper remedy for overconfidence. Let us by all means carry on the struggle to "save the environment" by all feasible steps. But let us not entertain misguided expectations about the prospects of success—expectations whose probable disappointment cannot but result in despondency, recrimination, and the tempting resort to the dire political measures that are natural to gravely disillusioned people.

The stance I see as necessary is not one of fatalistic resignation but of carrying on the good fight to save the environment—but doing so in fully realistic awareness that we are carrying on a limited war in which an actual victory may well lie beyond our grasp. It has taken an extraordinarily difficult struggle for us to arrive at a limited war perspective in international relations under the inexorable pressure of the political and technological facts of our times. And we have not even begun to move toward the corresponding mentality in the sphere of social problems and domestic difficulties. Yet just this—as I see it—is one of the crucial sociotechnological imperatives of our day.

CONCLUSION

The time has come for summing up. The conception that the quality of life—currently under threat by the environmental crisis—represents simply another one of those binds for which the welfare economists' classic prescription of "producing oneself out of it" seems to me profoundly misguided. In my discussion I have set before you the hypothesis of the environmental crisis as not really a crisis at all, but the inauguration of a permanent condition of things.

I have tried to argue that one of the main implications of this is a reversal of the ongoing escalation of expectations that is and long has been rife among Americans. In various crucial respects regarding the quality of life we just may have to settle for less. I have maintained that this development will exact from Americans a great price in terms of ideological revisionism. In particular, it will demand as victims our inclination to progressivism, our Promethean faith in man's technological omnipotence, and our penchant for millenial thinking. What is needed in the face of the environmental crises at this point, as I see it, may well be not a magisterial confidence that things can be put right, but a large dose of cool realism tempered with stoic resignation. We had better get used to the idea that we may have to scale down our expectations and learn to settle for less in point of standard of living and quality of life.

This conclusion will very likely strike many as a repulsive instance of "gloom and doom" thinking. This would be quite wrong. The moral, as I see it, is at worst one of gloom without doom. Man is a being of enormous adaptability, resiliency, and power. He has learned to survive and make the best of it under some extremely difficult and unpleasant conditions. By all means, let us do everything we can to save the environment. But if we do not do a very good job of it—and I for one do not think we will—it is not necessarily the end of the world. Let us not sell man short. We have been in some unpleasant circumstances before and have managed to cope.

A Philosopher Looks at the Population Bomb

ROBERT G. BURTON

ONE OF THE most widely read books focusing on the demographic component of the environmental crisis is Paul Ehrlich's *The Population Bomb*.[1] According to Ehrlich, the phrases "population bomb" and "population explosion" were first used in a pamphlet issued by the Hugh Moore Fund in 1954. Today these phrases are widely used, and there is no doubt that they have helped call attention to an extremely problematic situation. But to depict this situation as a time bomb with lighted fuse is misleading. No one really wants to suggest that we become preoccupied with speculation about a catastrophic event in the indefinite future, an event that may yet be prevented if the bomb is defused in time. The real concern is with a process that is already well under way, a process many of whose destructive effects are now history and as such irreversible. If a phrase with shock value is needed, "the population avalanche" would seem to be more apt.

To provide a rough sketch and defense of the philosophical perspective[2] from which I approach our central problem, I would begin with the fact that we as human beings have a variety of needs and wants, many of which we consciously and deliberately try to satisfy. Differences of taste and temperament and differences of talent and experience account, in large measure, for the fact that no two people seem to share identical sets of ends. But there are certain ends that virtually all of us share, and some of them, such as life, health, and security, are basic in the sense that without

1. Paul R. Ehrlich, *The Population Bomb* (New York: Ballantine, 1968).
2. This perspective reflects the influence of many philosophers past and present. Among contemporaries see for example: Kurt Baier, *The Moral Point of View* (Ithaca, N.Y.: Cornell University Press, 1958); William K. Frankena, *Ethics* (Englewood Cliffs, N.J.: Prentice-Hall, 1963); Alan Gewirth, *Political Philosophy* (New York: Macmillan, 1965); Michael Scriven, *Primary Philosophy* (New York: McGraw-Hill, 1966).

them it is either extremely difficult or impossible to obtain the others which normally include such intrinsic values as personal affection, aesthetic enjoyments, and the maximization of freedom. There is no single end such as the maximization of pleasure and the minimization of pain which all men, as a matter of psychological fact, seek and in relation to which all other ends have only instrumental value. And to my knowledge no ethicist has ever produced a compelling argument for the reduction of all intrinsic values to one or even to a specific finite set. It does seem clear to me that what we value intrinsically is not simply things as such but the experience of them. For example, the art collector does not buy painting X because he values X simpliciter but because he wants to own and contemplate at his pleasure, or display, or hoard, or make a gift of, or do something else with painting X. And finally, I believe that psychological egoism can be shown to be factually false. We sometimes do take an intrinsic, other-directed interest in the welfare or illfare of others; not all interests of the self are selfish interests.

It seems to me that the only compelling justification for living in society and for subscribing to the institutions of morality and law is the pragmatic justification which consists in showing that there is no rational alternative, assuming that there are various ends of the sort described above that we want to obtain by the best possible means. The argument may be sketched as follows. Suppose that you were stranded alone on a small, tropical island. If you wanted to continue to live for as long as possible and as well as possible, it would be irrational to begin working toward those ends by polluting the only source of potable water and destroying any vegetation that might otherwise provide food. Only a mad man or a complete fool would choose to be as irrational as possible in order to achieve his ends. Rationality is not the source of all other values, but given the fact that one has various primitive needs and wants, the rational approach is by definition the best way to go about satisfying them. But reason does not merely provide the most efficient means to particular ends, it also provides for the criticism of ends, and working together with taste, it enables one to choose between conflicting ends and to rank those that survive scrutiny in order of priority.

Moving from the artificial, desert island situation to the real, societal level of complexity, it is possible to view the institutions of morality and law as extensions of the rationality described above. When Nietzsche said that morality is only for the weak, Hobbes had long since observed that we are all weak in the relevant sense. The only alternative to society governed by the institutions of morality and law is anarchy in which life would be "solitary, poor, nasty, brutish, and short." In the *Republic*, Plato offers a similar justification for the mutual limitation of individual freedom involved in the establishment of these social institutions. In the alternative world in which everyone is completely free to do as he chooses, the evil that would result from being exploited by everyone else would far outweigh the good that would result from being able to exploit others with moral and legal impunity. It is the paradox of liberty that to maximize liberty, we must agree to limit it. For example, to maximize our freedom of travel by automobile, it is necessary to establish and observe a number of conventions that limit how, when, where, and what we may drive on the public highways. This example reminds us that there is much more than survival at issue here. In moving from a primitive subsistence economy to an agrarian economy, we began to find the necessary leisure for the intellectual pursuits that have improved the "spiritual" as well as the material quality of our lives. The automobile and the system of highways that we often take for granted are just one product of the agricultural and industrial revolutions that would have been impossible without society's division of labor and enormous potential for cooperative effort.

Society depends upon moral and legal conventions, and it is obvious that these conventions will work only if virtually all members of society are willing to abide by them. But one could scarcely hope to get anything approaching universal subscription to the moral and legal institutions if such subscription did not carry with it the promise of equal rights for all subscribers. Indeed it would be irrational to subscribe if by that very act one were to become a second-class citizen. And so I believe that one of the fundamental moral principles, the principle of distributive justice according to which we have a prima facie obligation to treat people equally, is justified by the fact that universal subscription to a system without such a principle would be irrational.

The other moral principle that I would regard as fundamental is the principle of beneficence or utility according to which we have a prima facie obligation to maximize the total amount of good in the world. This principle is grounded in the fact, noted at the outset, that we have a natural desire to satisfy a variety of fundamental needs and wants. If we had no such desire, if we had literally no natural inclination to achieve ends which we regard as good, it is doubtful that the principle of utility would ever have been formulated, and it is certain that there would be no compelling reason for adopting it. But before making some concluding observations about the relationship between the principles of utility and justice, I want to say a few things about the relationship between morality and law.

In the first place, both morality and law must be contrasted with mere prudentialism since both of them sometimes require that we put the interests of other people ahead of our own. For most of us, it would require a sacrifice of self-interest if we were to find a wallet containing a large sum of money and to return it to its owner in exchange for an expression of gratitude or a token reward. And the same holds for the young man who submits to the military draft or the automotive industry that reluctantly moves to reduce harmful exhaust emissions in compliance with the law.

The most salient features that distinguish morality from law are 1) that morality is neither created nor destroyed by legislative, executive, or judicial fiat and 2) that its only sanctions, in addition to the individual agent's desire to be moral, are informal expressions of approval and disapproval. It would be theoretically possible to have a society governed solely by morality, but there is nothing in our knowledge of human nature and history to suggest that such a system could actually work. At the opposite extreme, we could imagine a society in which every aspect of human conduct was governed by explicit laws, having as their effective sanctions the threat of fines, or imprisonment, or worse. It is doubtful that such an absolutely totalitarian system has ever been seriously advocated, and fortunately there is no more evidence for the viability of this horrifying system than for the viability of its beatific opposite. In reality we find ourselves somewhere in between these extremes; we find that the institution of morality must be reinforced to some extent by the institution of law. The chief task of political philosophy is to determine the extent and mode of this reinforcement. How should the governmental agencies that are to create and enforce the law be selected, what shall be the ends to which their political power is directed, and what limits shall be placed upon the means that they may employ to achieve those ends, or, to put the question differently, what human rights are exempt from governmental infringement? Only ends can justify means, but few if any ends justify any means whatever.

In conclusion, I would contend that the only adequate foundation for morality and law is the two, irreducible principles of utility and justice. The principle of utility provides for the maximization of a content that is good while the principle of justice provides the formula for its distribution. The principle of distributive justice with no goods to distribute is an empty formula. The principle of utility, untempered by the principle of justice, not only permits, but even requires, the exploitation of the innocent if such exploitation would yield maximum utility. When there is a conflict between utility and justice, morality usually requires that some utility be sacrificed in the interest of equal consideration for all. But unfortunately there are times when the rights of some must be sacrificed either to prevent some grave public evil or to secure some enormous public good. I need not labor the point that there are no infallible guides for resolving such conflicts of interest. We can, at best, try to make decisions that are based upon knowledge of the relevant facts and clarity of thought. But now, with a few philosophical tools at our disposal, let us turn our attention to the human-population problem.

The notion that there was once a natural ecological balance that was drastically upset only with the advent of man is largely a myth. Change is the law of life. It has been estimated that 99 percent of the forms of life that have ever existed on the earth are now extinct, and of these an estimated 95 percent achieved extinction without the help of man. Today there are more than one million identified species of plants and animals that inhabit the biosphere. And theoretically, any one of these species has the reproductive potential to overpopulate the world within a few generations. But in point of fact, this reproductive potential has always been regulated by such interrelated factors as the climate, a limited supply of food, competition with other species, and disease. No species has unlimited control over the environment, but man with his unique capacity for action based upon reflection and rational deliberation has certainly achieved dominance. So far as we know, man is the first species to face the responsibilty of deciding whether to become extinct. Extinction may not be inevitable, but there is biological limit to the number of humans our finite biosphere can support. The question is not whether we will reach zero population growth, but when and for what reasons.

There is also considerable controversy among professional environmentalists over which of two factors, the continuing population growth or a recklessly myopic technology, is most responsible for the environmental crisis. The neo-Malthusians, led by Paul Ehrlich, argue that the ever-growing demand for higher living standards inevitably leads to increased pollution and the eventual destruction of the environment. For these passionate prophets of doom, the threat of extinction through disease, famine, and war is now upon us. On the other side of the issue, those who find an ecologically faulty technology to be the major culprit tend to be less given to sensational exaggeration and more optimistic about the prospects for improving the situation. Men like Ansley Coale, Barry Commoner, and Phillip Hauser point out that in the last twenty-five years there has been a sharp rise in the per capita production of pollutants. This clearly indicates that even if we could reach zero population growth overnight, we would have only a partial solution to the problem. Much of the problem stems from the fact that until now we have encouraged continuous economic growth and development without taking into account its effect on the environment. We have treated clean air and clean water as free waste disposal systems. We are now aware of the fact that they are not free and that we must develop recycling procedures that enable us to add their cost to the total cost of production. This will obviously mean greater cost to the consumer, but there is no rational alternative. Ansley Coale has offered one very appealing, even if generally impractical, suggestion on how this might be accomplished, namely, by requiring those who use flowing water to take in the water downstream of their operation and discharge it upstream.[3]

No one knows how long modern man has inhabited the earth; estimates range from fifty thousand to two hundred thousand years. But we do know that until as recently as three hundred years ago, man's extremely high birth rate was controlled, as it is for all other species, by an almost equally high death rate. This extremely high death rate was brought about by the great Malthusian checks of disease and famine, and, to a much lesser extent, war. And the result was a growth rate only slightly above the replacement level. By most estimates it took until about two thousand years ago to achieve a human population of one-fourth billion and another sixteen centuries for that figure to double. But at that point, technological improvements in agriculture, the industrial revolution, significant advancements in the control of disease, and accelerated expansion into a new world rich with additional resources began to effect a sharp decline in the death rate that was not accompanied by a comparable decline in the birth rate. The well-known result was a geometric increase in the rate of growth of the human population. In only two centuries the population had doubled, and at the present rate of growth our current world population of approximately three and one-half billion will double in about thirty-five years.

With the sharp decline in the death rate of the westerner there was a striking increase in life expectancy which had, for centuries, been no more than thirty to thirty-five years. By the beginning of this century, our life expectancy was forty-five to fifty years, and today it is approximately seventy years. The non-Western masses of the world did not really begin to share in this increased longevity until the period following the Second World War when Western medicine was introduced on a massive scale. Since that time there has been a continued depression of death rates with no significant reduction in the habitual birth rates.

Now we noted earlier that since the resources of the biosphere are limited, zero population growth is inevitable. The only question is whether it will be achieved by birth control or by death

3. Ansley J. Coale, "Man and His Environment," *Science* 170 (9 October 1970): 132.

control; either the birth rate must go down or the death rate must go back up. Now there is no question in my mind of which is preferable. And I suspect that most of the thoughtful citizens of the developed countries of the world would agree with me. If we take the initiative we can continue to achieve much more than mere survival. But the masses of the people in the underdeveloped countries of Asia, Africa, and Latin America have maintained such high birth rates in the face of such widespread hunger and abject poverty that one wonders whether they have ever seen the connection between the two. Efforts to introduce birth control methods have made little impact and are not likely to succeed as long as the level of motivation is low and the rate of illiteracy very high. Faced with this very depressing situation, we are finally coming to realize that our ability to help these underdeveloped countries is very limited. Most forms of aid have only served to increase both dependency and the rate of population growth which means that in the long run, barring drastic changes from within, the inevitable Malthusian consequences will be even more severe. It is now clear that only aid that promotes self-help will have lasting value. One form of aid that shows some promise is the loan of plant geneticists who have helped such countries set up breeding programs resulting in hybrids that give much higher grain yields.

I conclude this brief discussion of the plight of the underdeveloped countries by raising the question of our moral responsibility in this matter. Many would argue that countries do not have moral obligations to other countries, and I am willing to concede the point. But one might still ask whether the principle of equal consideration for all does not require the individual to make as great an effort on behalf of every Indian or every Latin American as he makes on behalf of the people with whom he actually lives and works or the members of his family. The obvious answer to this question is that it would be impossible to spread oneself so thinly. The practical effect of even trying would be that no one would benefit. "Ought" implies "can." I can normally do the most good by concentrating the major portion of my efforts on that relatively small number of people whose needs and wants I understand best.

For the remainder of this paper I will examine briefly the relationship between population growth in the United States and the environmental crisis. With a population of slightly over two hundred million, and a growth rate that would, if not reduced, cause us to double this figure in about seventy years, our population problem is, in one sense, the most serious in the world. With only 6 percent of the world's population we consume on the order of 50 percent of the world's resources, some of which, notably the fossil fuels, are nonrenewable. Economists tend to reject the implication that we are depriving the underdeveloped countries of the basis for their future development by using up their resources. They argue that only by exporting their raw materials can these countries afford to import the necessary capital equipment for economic development. There is undoubtedly some merit to this argument, but it is only fair to observe that in many of the countries that provide us with resources there is, as yet, little evidence that they have benefited significantly. It sometimes seems that the great discrepancy between the low price of raw materials and the high price of finished goods is the contemporary equivalent of colonial exploitation.

Another factor that contributes to both environmental and human stress is the distribution of our population. Indeed, many demographers consider this factor to be more important at this stage in our history than either the total size of our population or its rate of growth. Our urban blight is an intolerable disgrace.

The standard demographer's objection to the immediate attainment of zero population growth is the effect that this would have on the composition of our population. Because of the postwar baby boom there are at present a large number of women entering the childbearing years who would be limited to having only a little over one child per family for a period of approximately fifteen years. The resultant shortage of young people would cause such a disruption in our educational and other social institutions that the benefit would not be worth the cost. Of course it goes without saying that even if the public benefit justified the cost, it would be highly unlikely that one could persuade the mothers involved to settle for one child when the latest surveys indicate that they still want an average of three. The best solution would seem to be to attempt to get couples to settle for an average of two children so that there would be a gradual leveling of the growth rate. If we could "power down" to an average of two children per family within the present decade and then maintain this level of fertility and if we could also equalize the immigration-emigration rate, then we would reach zero population growth in fifty to sixty years with a total population of something less than four hundred million people. At that time we would have a median age of thirty-seven years as opposed to our current median age of twenty-eight years. This change in median age would mean that much more attention would have to be devoted to improving the quality of life for the aged.

But what are we to conclude from all of this, and what ought we to do about it? In discussing human population growth and some of its implications for the environmental crisis, I have been able to touch on but few points. I have contrasted the plight of some of the underdeveloped countries, whose populations seem destined to continue to be controlled by the classical biological factors, with the plight of a country such as ours in which such control does not appear to be inevitable, at least not yet. I have tried to suggest that since there is very little that we *can* do, either as a nation or as individuals, that will really help countries like India, there is very little that we *ought* to do. What becomes of India and other countries like it will no doubt affect all of us to some degree; it is possible that an epidemic or plague could start in India and eventually reach the other continents. But even if we were virtually isolated from direct involvement with her, we would not enjoy watching her starve to death. And yet, there is literally no way that we can feed or otherwise save her. In the very long run, all men must find ways to cooperate if any are to survive. But in the short run there is little evidence to suggest that we are either sufficiently concerned about the welfare of all men or sufficiently rational to make more than token progress at the international level. And so it would seem wise to concentrate most of one's efforts within one's own country where these efforts have some chance of success. Perhaps the best way to educate the poorer countries of the world is by setting a good example for them to follow.

In conclusion then, what ought we to do in our own country? I have tried to suggest that our own population growth rate is but one of many factors that require rational control. As I indicated above, I believe that it is in the general interest for us to modify our economic practices so as to include the cost of waste disposal and the recycling of such resources as air and water in the total cost of production. This would amount to the tempering of the profit motive by the principle of equal rights for all.

And finally, if we can agree that the relatively gradual way of reaching zero population growth described above is in the general interest, how can we get couples to begin having an average of only two children? There are two main possibilities. There are those who believe that if we could just develop and distribute freely the perfect contraceptive, the birth rate would almost immediately reach the replacement level. Would that this were so! The fact is that repeated surveys have shown that even if all of the unwanted children could be eliminated, too many people still want three children. What is obviously needed is a change of attitude. This is not to minimize the importance of continuing the search for the perfect contraceptive. And to be sure, no one has yet offered a compelling reason why all methods of birth control, including legalized abortion, should not be freely available. But within the limits of the morally and legally acceptable, what can be done to change the number of children that people want?

I have already contended that the institutions of morality and law were made to serve man and not vice versa. I have also suggested that our government of laws is essentially a reinforcement to morality improving our chances of doing two things, (1) maximizing good, particularly those goods that require large scale cooperative efforts, and (2) achieving social justice defined as equality of opportunity or consideration for all citizens. For example, to combat blatant injustice, the force of law was required to integrate the high school in Little Rock, Arkansas. At the time, it was argued that such legal action would have no effect on the racist attitudes that were at the root of the problem. Now it is true that the law can only regulate conduct directly and not attitudes. Nevertheless, a study of attitudes in the Little Rock High School after ten years of forced integration showed that there had been a dramatic change. In short, by regulating conduct, the law can indirectly influence attitudes. But what should be the government's role vis-à-vis the population problem? Is the situation comparable? Where is the blatant injustice? Should all parents who have more than two children be singled out for official government censure. I think not; I think that such suggestions are alien to our whole concept of government and its *raison d'être.*

The gentlest form of governmental incentive that has been seriously proposed to date is a revision of our tax laws to discourage rather than encourage large families. It would seem possible to devise laws that would not hurt those at the poverty level who pay few taxes anyway and make a relatively small contribution to the overall population growth while requiring the middle-class Americans whose large families make greater demands on the environment to shoulder a somewhat larger portion of the tax burden. But I suspect that things would have to appear much more desperate than they now appear for our legislators to make those revisions.

In the final analysis we must begin by changing our own attitudes, and then through moral suasion and example attempt to influence the attitudes of others. If we become convinced that our welfare and the welfare of our children depend on our learning to want less, to consume less, and to waste less, then we will have some chance of success. During the depression and without the aid of the perfect contraceptive, there was a drop in the birth rate to near replacement level which reflected the fact that Americans were willing to do what was necessary to provide a better life for themselves and their children. Can we do any less?

The Big Thicket: A Case Study in Attitudes toward Environment

PETE A. Y. GUNTER

THE SOUTHEASTERN EVERGREEN FOREST sweeps westward from southern Virginia through the Carolinas and Georgia. To the east it reaches down to central Florida and to the west into the highly divergent geographical accident of Texas.[1] At its southwesternmost tip, just before the beginnings of Texas's dry post oak woods and blackland prairies, it forms a region of tangled undergrowth, deep woods, and remarkable variety. This region—an ecotone within an ecotone—is called the Big Thicket.

Pioneers heading out from Louisiana into southeast Texas in the 1820s found their way blocked time and again by junglelike growth bordering meandering streams. The forbidding woods stretched monotonously from horizon to horizon, showing no sign of break or opening. Under a thick canopy of pine and magnolia there was black shade at noon; panthers screamed at night in trackless swamps. The settlers called the impassable area the Big Thicket, and advised travelers to give it a wide berth. Thanks to twin accidents of war and geographic isolation, it was to remain wild into the twentieth century. I used to hunt and fish there as a boy.

Originally the Big Thicket covered around three and one-half million acres[2] and stretched west from just within the Louisiana border over a hundred miles of southeast Texas, ending some miles south of the present town of Conroe, thirty-five miles north of Houston.[3] It paralleled the Gulf Coast from thirty to sixty miles

1. Pierre Dansereau, *Biogeography, An Ecological Perspective* (New York: Ronald Press, 1957), pp. 64–65. The Thicket is also at the southwestern limit of two further southeastern forest communities, oak-pine and oak-hickory.

2. H. B. Parks and V. L. Cory, *Biological Survey of the East Texas Big Thicket Area*, 2d ed. (Huntsville, Tex.: Sam Houston Press, 1938), p. 4.

3. Claude A. McLeod, *The Big Thicket of East Texas* (Huntsville, Tex.: Sam Houston Press, 1967), pp. 14–15.

inland and was approximately sixty miles in width at its widest point. When the first settlers found the "Thicket" it was, therefore, roughly half the size of Maryland, or as large as Connecticut. To-day it is immeasurably reduced in size, and a heated controversy continues over attempts to rescue its remainder.

Ecotones are regions of transition. They are of interest to biologists because of what they can teach us about the nature of biotic communities and their interrelations. By saying that the Big Thicket is an "ecotone within an ecotone" one means that it is in two different respects a region of transition. Most obviously, it is a place where eastern and western biotic communities meet, but it is also a bridge between temperate and subtropical vegetation. Water tupelo and baldcypress grow there, but so do western tumbleweed and mesquite. Its hillslopes reproduce plant growth patterns common to the Appalachian highlands, hundreds of miles away; its flatlands resemble jungles in the Mexican states of Tamaulipas and Vera Cruz. It is notable for its orchids and palmetto thickets, but it is equally notable as the far southwestern distribution limit of beech trees and sugar maple. The variety exhibited by its plant life is exhibited by its animal life as well. Roadrunners dart along its sandy roads, and roseate spoonbills and water turkeys nest in its river bottoms. The Louisiana black bear is still seen there, as is the ring-tailed cat, a desert species whose easternmost distribution is reached in the Thicket counties.[4] "You can find anything in there," the old settlers drawled, "from an elephant to a cricket." Allowances made for rhetoric, they were more right than they knew. The Big Thicket is the biological crossroads of North America.

The Big Thicket, however, is more than a crossroads: it is an *intensification* of plant and animal life as well. The lushness of its plant life has a simple geological explanation. Not many thousands of years ago the present Thicket region was an inland arm of the Gulf of Mexico into which ancestors of present-day rivers poured rich alluvial wastes.[5] As the waters receded, sand dunes

4. William B. Davis, *The Mammals of Texas* (Austin: Texas Parks and Wildlife Department, 1966), pp. 84–86.
5. H. B. Parks, "The Big Thicket," *Texas Geographic Magazine* 2, no. 1 (Summer 1938): 16–28.

became hills, brackish ponds swamps, and sandbars, flatlands. The rich water-bearing loams of the "fossil seabottom" became carpeted with a profusion of herbaceous plants and trees which thrived there. Today in spite of unlimited timbering, thirteen trees in the area are known to be the largest of their species in the world;[6] thirty-five of Texas's largest trees-in-their-species are found there as well.[7] Pecan trees there reach the stature of douglas firs; bald cypress reach the size of redwoods. One cypress there was recently certified to be the tallest in the world. The Big Thicket is thus a "sudden flourishing of junglelike growth"[8] just before the edge of the Southern woodlands. It is a biological garden as well as a biological crossroads.[9]

An area which enjoys the blessings of ecological diversity, botanical richness, and geographic isolation is admirably suited to function as a refugium. Increasingly this has been so. Indians long ago sought shelter there; today Texas's only Indian reservation is on the Thicket's northern edge.[10] The Texas red wolf (*Canis rufus*), dangerously reduced in numbers, lairs on the prairies at

6. National "champion trees" in the Big Thicket include: black hickory, American holly, Texas honeylocust, pyramid magnolia, Mexican plum, redbay, eastern redcedar, tree sparkleberry, western soapberry, Chinese tallowtree, bluejack oak, longleaf pine, and Yaupon. (This list is valid as of 1 October 1969.) Certified near-champions in the area include: water elm, planertree, sweetbay, water tupelo, sugar hackberry, common sweetleaf, Allegheny chinkapin, and two-wing silverbell.

7. State "champion trees" include white ash, American basswood (linden), American beech, river birch, Carolina laurelcherry, flowering dogwood, hercules clud, black hickory, mockernut hickory, shagbark hickory, water hickory, American holly, honeylocust, Texas honeylocust, Eastern hophornbeam, American hornbeam, pyramid magnolia, southern magnolia, blackjack oak, laurel oak, shumard oak, swamp chestnut oak, cherrybark oak, white oak, loblolly pine, longleaf pine, slash pine, Mexican plum, redbay, eastern redbud, eastern redcedar, two winged silverbell, tree sparkleberry, sugarberry (sugar hackberry), sweetbay, sweetgum, common sweetleaf, American sycamore, Chinese tallowtree, yaupon, and water tupelo.

8. Dr. Donovan Correll, Texas Research Institute, at Big Thicket senate hearings, April 1970.

9. "I expected an entirely junglelike growth, where passageway would have to be hacked with a machete. There are still many such spots in the Thicket but in its opened up, road-riddled state today, it resembles most of all a giant wild garden that is being looted and despoiled." Mary Lasswell, *I'll Take Texas* (Boston: Houghton Mifflin, 1958), p. 231.

10. W. E. S. Folsum-Dickerson, *The White Path* (San Antonio, Tex.: Naylor, 1965).

the Thicket's southern extreme.[11] The ivory-billed woodpecker, long thought to be extinct, has been reported in the bottomlands along the Neches River over the last few years, though efforts to achieve a definitive sighting have failed. Bachman's warbler, America's rarest songbird, is found there, along with the scarce red-cockaded woodpecker. The golden eagle is regularly shot there.[12] The bald eagle is a possible resident. The region hosts over three hundred species of birds,[13] along with one thousand varieties of flowering plants. Among these are over thirty varieties of orchids,[14] as well as four of North America's five varieties of insect-eating plants.[15] Orchids and insectivores are becoming increasingly scarce in Texas as their habitats are destroyed. The Thicket will almost certainly be the "last stand" of many such plants in the Southwest, as the twin tides of urbanization and technology continue to rise in the region.

The character of the Thicket is further complicated by the introduction of "exotics," that is, plants and animals originally established elsewhere. My favorite story in this regard concerns a Houston businessman who some years ago turned loose an Australian wolfhound on a lonely Thicket road; subsequently backwoods settlers have seen the huge animal leading a wolfpack.[16] Equally interesting, a colony of squirrel monkeys, introduced from no one knows where,[17] was discovered not long ago living in the region. Razorback hogs ("piney woods rooters") roam the woods, along with packs of wild dogs; local stockmen have loosed herds of jackasses in the Thicket. Similarly for plant life. Throughout

11. Ronald M. Nowak, "Report on the Red Wolf," *Defenders of Wildlife News*, 45, no. 1 (January–February–March 1970): 82–94. The Texas red wolf is the rarest mammal in the United States.

12. The most recent case occurred in early January 1971. (Cf. *Kountze News*, 4 January 1971).

13. The Thicket is at the juncture of the eastern and western "Gulf flyways." In large measure this accounts for its unusually varied collection of migratory birds.

14. Most articles report around twenty varieties. With the help of Geraldine Watson of Silsbee and Dr. Donovan Correll, however, I have been able to verify between thirty and thirty-five varieties.

15. Namely: pitcher plant, bog violet, sundew, and several varieties of bladderwort. Venus flytrap is lacking.

16. Dempsie Henley, *The Murder of Silence: The Big Thicket Story* (Waco, Tex.: Texian Press, 1970), p. 176.

17. Henley, *Murder of Silence*, p. 177.

the Thicket you will find Chinese tallowtrees and mimosas, native to Southeast Asia. In one area there is a forest of cape jasmine extending over countless acres. No one knows where it came from.

As of this writing, a bill to establish a Big Thicket National Park lies ensconced in a congressional committee.[18] Such a bill is fully justified: failure not to salvage the last remnants of the once-mighty wilderness would be a national disgrace. What is at issue in this essay, however, is not the conservation of a region, but the destructive acts which have reduced it to a remnant and the attitudes or presuppositions which have made this reduction possible. The destruction of the Big Thicket will be presented in the following pages as an Ecological Melodrama in Four Acts.

Before setting the stage for the melodrama—or tragedy—a few remarks are called for. Admittedly, the subject matter has limitations. It does not provide direct insight into problems of urban and suburban development, of failing power sources, air pollution, or effects of psychological stress due to population density. The Big Thicket provides a paradigm case of preurban or even preindustrial environmental degeneration. I will argue, however, that such paradigm cases have much to teach us, in spite of their limitations.

A second and more subtle difficulty is also presented by the example chosen. One of the fundamental theoretical directions of the present environmental movement, as of the science of ecology, is a tendency toward holism, that is, the notion that "the whole is greater than the sum of its parts," or, put in terms of division rather than composition, that "the part takes on special characteristics through its relations to the whole."[19] The opposite of holism will in this essay be termed "atomism." In matters environmental, atomistic thinking is dangerously one-sided. Yet this essay must to some extent commit the sin of atomism, simply by the fact that it isolates a single reality (the Big Thicket) as if it somehow existed alone, in and for itself. The artificiality of such an approach can only be excused if the history of the region in ques-

18. Committee on Interior and Insular Affairs, Wayne Aspinal, chairman.
19. "It is the total impact of all factors that conditions the nature of the community, its structure, composition and dynamics. Even though individual factors and elements can be shown to exert a limiting and even a controlling influence . . . the biocenosis has a wholeness which is organismic and not strictly reducible to the sum of its parts." Dansereau, *Biogeography*, p. 124.

tion mirrors the history of the American environment generally and is so thoroughly interrelated with that history that there can be no question but what it exhibits main features of an unconscious but thoroughly operative philosophy of nature. This essay is an attempt to see a particular region as a whole, to relate it to an environing complex of factors dating back into the shadows of history, and to draw from the resulting picture some insights relevant to the entire present and the total future. A philosopher of the environment need not limit himself to less. At least, he could not do more.

DESTRUCTION IN FOUR ACTS

In his First Antinomy, Kant poses the question whether the world in space and time is finite or infinite. Pure reason, it would seem, cannot answer this question. The pioneers, however, had no difficulty with it; they saw nature as infinite. Moreover, the great majority of them regarded infinite nature as a domain to be exploited. Into the Infinite Nature of the South the trapper, the trader, the backwoodsman, plunged headlong, trailed by the planter and lumberman and, finally, by the builders of towns and cities. Each carved out his own atom of progress. The biological wealth and stability of the South, like that of the nation generally, steadily declined.

The earliest wave of immigrants, as has already been noted, by-passed the Thicket. Only gradually did settlers filter into the dense woods, and these managed only minor alterations in the region's ecology. Many of them, in the words of J. Frank Dobie, wanted to forget and be forgotten;[20] the rest confined themselves to a modest "take" from the rich timberlands. By the Civil War, only a few villages, some farms, and a handful of plantations spotted the Thicket, which became the successful sanctuary of innumerable Confederate deserters (or Union sympathizers, depending on one's viewpoint) in spite of determined attempts by Confederate troops to drive them out.[21] During the same years, the East Texas Rail-

20. J. Frank Dobie, *The Ben Lilly Legend* (Boston: Little, Brown and Company, 1950), pp. 104–105.
21. On one occasion the Confederates tried unsuccessfully to drive the "Jayhawkers" out of hiding with a carefully set forest fire. For over one-half

road was dismantled and fed into the Confederate war effort, with the result that logging railroads did not appear in the sprawling Thicket until the 1880s.[22] Even by the 1890s the railroads reached only the western regions of the wilderness. Not until the turn of the century, in fact, did logging railroads and their branch lines make a frontal assault on the Thicket's eastern reaches. Old men today can still recall this last primitive wilderness.

The first stage of environmental transformation in the region (1820–1885), therefore, resulted in minimal deterioration, but the second (1885–1915) resulted in massive destruction:

> Never before nor since have men so quickly and ruthlessly "slashed" a forest as they did the Southern coniferous forest, the most extensive of its kind. Rebel or Yankee, the Southern lumber baron operated under a "cut and get out" policy. Labor was cheap and plentiful, the terrain flat to gently rolling, and the weather never severe.[23]

As Dempsie Henley relates in his book, *The Murder of Silence*, much of the timberland in the Big Thicket was stolen, pure and simple. Taking advantage of Texas's "use and possession" laws, corporate interests put in "push roads" and felled adjacent timber often before the settler, in whose family the land had been for two or three generations, was even aware the damage had been done. Objectors were met at the courthouse by corporation lawyers quoting eloquent Latin. The settlers, angry and embittered, fought back with the only means at their disposal: they burned down the forests being seized from them.[24]

It does not follow from the fact that there was friction between lumber interests and small landowners over the cutting of timber that the root concepts of either group toward environment differed significantly. Pioneer attitudes and those of corporate capitalism complemented each other; the latter could scarcely have existed in its historically familiar form without the connivance of the

---

century nothing would grow on Kaiser's Burnout as the hundred-plus acres of charred stumps and heat-fused sand came to be called.

22. McLeod, *The Big Thicket of East Texas*, pp. 4–5.

23. Reuben L. Parsons, quoted in Ruth A. Allen, *East Texas Lumber Workers, An Economic and Social Picture, 1870–1950* (Austin: University of Texas Press, 1961), p. 19.

24. Henley, *Murder of Silence*, pp. 14–15.

former.[25] The major difference was simply that the lumber companies operated on a grander scale than the settlers, and with a more advanced technology. There was, however, one minor difference. The settler viewed his homestead and its immediate environs as something inviolable. His feelings in this respect were and still are in some places the only block in the way of the wholesale leveling of the forests.

Such a block could make little difference in the Big Thicket counties, where as much as 84 percent of the land came to be lumber-company owned. One searches in vain, amid the ensuing decimation, for a single virgin grove, swamp, baygall,[26] or giant tree bypassed, or natural game sanctuary left intact. The last first-growth timber (with few notable exceptions) was cut by the 1920s; during the same years bear, panther, and even deer became virtually extinct.[27] One of the richest biological areas in the northern hemisphere had been turned in two and one-half decades into a forest of stumps—stumps and struggling saplings. Ironically this transformation coincided with the birth of the "First Conservation Movement" in the United States. The Southern Evergreen Forest was slashed, unnoticed, as Teddy Roosevelt and Gifford Pinchot formulated our first national environmental policies.

In 1927 a Big Thicket Association was formed, which contributed materially to the first and (to date) only biological survey of the area and which, for a brief period in the late 1930s, seemed perilously close to bringing state and local political leaders around to the idea of a Big Thicket National Park.[28] The Second World War intervened, however, and the hopes of conservationists crumbled. It was not until the 1950s that attention could be focused again on the wilderness. By the time a second Big Thicket Association could be founded, time was running out. This period (1915–

25. Walter Prescott Webb, *The Great Frontier* (London: Secker and Warburg, 1953).

26. A swamp community composed of bay trees (*Magnolia virginiana*) and gallberry bushes.

27. During the 1930s one last doe was discovered in east Texas near the Louisiana border. Several hundred hunters gathered with countless dogs to hunt the creature down—with wonderful success. Present deer in the area were introduced by state wildlife officials.

28. Cf. *Beaumont Enterprise*, 29 April 1939; *Beaumont Business*, May 1938; *Dallas Morning News*, 19 October 1937; *Houston Chronicle*, 2 January 1955.

1950) constitutes the third phase of environmental decline, and coincides, more or less, with the birth and death of the original Big Thicket Association. The fourth stage (1950 to the present) contains not only the birth of the second Big Thicket Association but a growing awareness, nationally, of the plight of the threatened region.

If the villain of the second act is the lumber baron, the villain of the third is the oil company. Oil strikes began along the southern margin of the region shortly after 1900 and continued sporadically thereafter, with predictably negative results. Slush pits, overflow ponds, oilfield roads were followed by the construction of countless oil pipelines which now crisscross the Thicket in every direction. Pipeline corridors are about the width of a football field and are laid out without reference to ecological boundaries. Whoever thinks that oil operations pose no threat to Alaska ought to study long and hard the results of oil operations in the Thicket.[29] I particularly recommend a hike down Pine Island Bayou, where saltwater overflow from oil wells has killed every cypress for twenty miles.

For those who have followed closely, there must seem to be a striking inconsistency in the narrative so far. For if the Big Thicket has already been "slashed," how can there be a dispute over "saving" it? The contradiction, however, is only apparent. Fifty to sixty-five inches of annual rainfall and a subtropical climate make possible the rapid regrowth of sizable portions of the wilderness which, deprived of its overstory of shade-tolerant hardwoods, gives birth to an amazing tangle of vines, shrubs, and saplings.[30] Into this environment deer, bobcats, foxes, even bear and panther return. The old forest types slowly assert themselves. As late as the 1950s prisoners from the nearby Huntsville penitentiary headed toward the Thicket to hide. Stories of hermits subsisting there for years on a diet of armadillos and wild berries are common.[31]

---

29. Particularly obvious is the acreage of dead trees left around oilfield operations in the area and the sludge-filled ditches around oilfields—ditches which were formerly creeks.

30. Much of the region's thickest vegetation in fact consists of inferior "disclimax" vegetation which bears no resemblance to the Big Thicket's original condition.

31. Francis E. Abernethy, ed., *Tales From the Big Thicket* (Austin: University of Texas Press, 1966), pp. 11–12.

It is, then, over the reborn Thicket wilderness that the present struggle is being waged. There is a great deal to be learned from the nature and the direction of this struggle. When the second Big Thicket Association was first established in 1964, attempts were made to discredit it with rumors.[32] If a park were created, children would be eaten by bears, old people would lose their farms, schools would be closed, visitors would come and "take over" local homes. When rumors died out, high cash bids were offered for discrediting information (fiscal irresponsibility, infidelity, Communist contacts) about Association members. Finally, fraudulent charges of perversion were brought against a prominent conservationist.[33] When the charges were thrown out of court the park stood acquitted of moral turpitude. Entrenched interests, however, tried a new tack; namely, ecological vandalism. Probably the most famous case of vandalism is that of the Judging Tree, as reported by Berton Roueché in the *New Yorker*.[34] The Judging Tree was a huge magnolia, estimated to be the oldest in the United States, whose three trunks pointed toward each of the three counties at whose juncture it stood. When conservationists took visiting dignitaries in to see it some five years ago, they found it dead. It had, they discovered, been poisoned: drilled in five places and injected with arsenate of lead. Lumber companies, questioned about the incident, replied they had never heard of the tree.[35] Meanwhile it was gone; there were, and are, no others to replace it.

Not long before this incident a well-known Thicket guide, Lance Rosier, had come across a heron rookery filled with dead birds. The rookery, Rosier explained, had been bombed from the air with insecticides. It was no accident: the rookery was clearly visible from the air, and markedly different from the surrounding terrain. Both the rookery and the Judging Tree, Rosier insisted, were warnings against those who wanted a park in the area. He was unquestionably correct.

32. P. A. Y. Gunter, "Reflections on a Stuffed Bird and The Big Thicket," *Defenders of Wildlife News* 43, no. 2 (April–May–June 1968): 185.

33. Gunter, "Reflections on a Stuffed Bird," p. 186.

34. Berton Roueché, "The Witness Tree," *New Yorker*, 30 August 1968, pp. 56–64.

35. The remark was somewhat less than honest. Lumber companies keep detailed records of large trees on or near their lands.

During this same period Prof. Claude McLeod[36] published a pamphlet analyzing the ecology of the Big Thicket and detailing its probable boundaries. The Thicket, he explained, was an area of rich, sandy loams supporting an overstory of three distinctive trees: magnolia, loblolly pines, and beech.[37] The publication of Professor McLeod's study was followed by an acceleration of cutting schedules, as slow-growing magnolias began disappearing from the region at a record pace. (Supreme Court Justice William O. Douglas and Sen. Ralph W. Yarborough even noticed on a tour of the Thicket that some of the magnolias cut were on public right of ways.) When conservationists complained, lumber company experts explained there was an increased market demand for timber.[38] That seemed unlikely: the main product of magnolia is railroad ties. In railroad ties a one-hundred-year-old magnolia is worth about $3.75.

Vandalism, however, finally managed to do what the conservationists could not; it created a public outcry. Lumber interests, sensing unfamiliar pressures, then made a highly effective compromise move, proposing a thirty-five-thousand-acre national monument against Sen. Ralph Yarborough's projected one-hundred-thousand-acre national park. The monument was to be composed of ten widely separated areas, exhibiting a variety of ecosystems. Hardly had the Department of the Interior selected the areas to be preserved when news came that one (a first-growth beech forest) was being cut by a private lumber operator; when it was gone, a second, still larger virgin beech grove selected for the monument was cut, while plans were announced to cut the last original loblolly pines in the area.[39] This vandalism was thor-

36. McLeod, *The Big Thicket of East Texas.*

37. McLeod, to be precise, distinguishes two distinct forest communities: an "Upper Thicket" comprised of magnolia, loblolly pine, and beech, and a "Lower Thicket" in which beech is replaced by swamp chestnut oak due to the acid, poorly-drained soils.

38. Dennis Farney, "Deciding on a 'Last True Wilderness,'" *Wall Street Journal*, 1 July 1968.

39. The units originally suggested for the national monument were: (1) Big Thicket Profile Unit (18,180 acres), (2) Beech Creek Unit (6,100 acres), (3) Neches Bottom Unit (3,040 acres), (4) Tanner Bayou Unit (4,800 acres), (5) Hickory Creek Savannah Unit (220 acres), (6) Beaumont Unit (1,700 acres), (7) Little Cypress Creek Unit (860 acres), (8) Loblolly Unit (550 acres), (9) Clear Fork Bog Unit (50 acres).

oughly legal. But it provoked the ire of the federal government *and* some local newspapers, forcing the lumber companies to invoke a moratorium on cutting in the involved areas. The moratorium has, by and large, been observed.[40]

The cutting moratorium was a great victory for conservationists. Its end results, however, were not quite what conservationists expected. The publicity which the dispute had created drew vacation subdivisions to the Thicket. These were built, usually, near watercourses and in the densest woods. Thus some of the most valuable botanical areas in the region have been singled out and destroyed by real-estate promoters. One of these was a further unit proposed for inclusion in the national monument; the verdant, untouched area has now been turned into a horrendous travesty by the name of Hoop 'n Holler Estates.[41] There, for scant money down, one can enjoy what advertising circulars proclaim as "life in a real wilderness."

Around six months ago I became lost while hiking along Pine Island Bayou in the heart of the traditional Thicket. Toward sundown I finally "came out" at a small frame house in the woods:

"What in tarnation were you doing' out there?" asked a youngish man driving a pickup.

"Uh—I'm looking for the ivory-billed woodpecker."

"Well," he snorted, "I'm lookin' for Jesus myself."

There was silence. Birds piped in the shadowy sprawl of palmetto and swamp oak. Why, he asked finally, was everyone so excited about a woodpecker? I explained that the ivory-bill was North America's largest woodpecker, bigger than a good-sized hawk and twice as gaudy, and now nearly extinct. How, I complained, could it continue to exist if the lumber companies kept cutting out the thickest, deepest timber along the bayous I had just seen? Why did they cut out all the cypress and magnolia?

40. There is a possible exception along Pine Island Bayou in the Profile Unit where big cypress have been cut. The question in this instance is the precise date of the cutting. Lumber companies control only 17,800 of the acres concerned. In the remaining areas countless acres have been cut by private owners.

41. A publication of the Wiggins Land Company of Livingston, Texas, lists some nineteen subdivisions under construction in the Big Thicket area.

"Hell," he answered, "it's their land isn't it?"

"Well . . . it's not that simple."

"Hell," he replied, "they ought to push down all that old stuff back in there. They ought to bulldoze it all down."

It was twilight; the wind was moving in the tops of the pines and the night hawks were soaring.

"It's an open secret," he nodded. "The lumber companies are trying to wreck all this country through here so they can't get it in the park. Everybody knows it. I've worked for those companies."

He took me up the rutted sand road in the back of the rusty pickup, let me off on the highway, and turned back. In the dusk the night-hawks spiraled.

Today in the Big Thicket, lumber companies are sending men in to girdle every hardwood tree on their lands, even on wet soil where pulp pines will never grow. Still worse, they are stripping twenty to thirty thousand acres of Big Thicket per year, even to the point of pulverizing root networks two or three feet beneath the surface. On these new clay prairies are planted geometrical rows of pines. A biological desert thus replaces a botanical garden.[42] Lumber companies blindly argue that no other course for them is economically feasible. But should a pine disease arise for which there is no immediate remedy, little would be left of the new pine plantations but grass and rotting trees. The fourth act of the Big Thicket Ecological Melodrama will therefore be the last. Everything not saved in the prospective national park will be turned, eventually, into tree farms and subdivisions. There will be no regrown Big Thicket this time.

THE PARADIGMS OF EXPLOITATION

The preceding account of the characters and disappearance of a unique area is necessarily schematic. Nonetheless, it should prove useful in illustrating some basic contentions about reigning at-

---

42. "If there are any birds in there," a biologist of my acquaintance quipped, "they'd better be carrying knapsacks. There's nothing in there for them to eat."

titudes toward our environment—illustrating them, and up to a point verifying them. The villains who have presided over the dismemberment of the Big Thicket have, with few exceptions, thought of themselves not as villains but as heroes, carrying out the dictates of a higher, or at least shrewder, wisdom. Their behavior suggests what they conceived this wisdom to be. We can read their *theorie* in their *praxis*.

In piecing together this theory it will be useful to resort to three general concepts: infinity, atomistic structure, and manipulability. Each of these concepts will be subject to further elucidation in terms of a second trilogy: space, time, and "matter."[43] Thus the assumption that the environment is infinite involves not only a belief in its spatial and temporal infinity but a faith in the virtual inexhaustibility of its contents. The belief that the environment can be understood atomistically involves not only a temporal and "material" atomism but a spatial atomism which presumes that events happening at one place do not essentially involve events happening elsewhere. The presumption that the environment can be manipulated ad infinitum equally involves a specific view of space, time, and their "contents." In treating all of these concepts, illustrations will be drawn from the history of the Big Thicket. It is hoped that the particularity of the examples will not detract from the broad generality of the conclusions drawn.

That men know the world is round by no means prevents them from thinking that it is infinite. The world began to appear spatially infinite at almost the same time that the Copernican conception of a spherical (hence finite) earth began to find favor. In the case of the Thicket, just as the settler felt there was always some farther "place" to go to if he wished, so the lumberman believed there was always some other place, farther on, where timber awaited him. The same complex of ideas reinforced, and was reinforced by, the notion that the "world" is temporally infinite: that is, that its environmental systems can endure indefinitely under sustained assault. The Thicket hunters who casually burned hundreds of acres to smoke out a raccoon[44] apparently believed that the woods could at best be destroyed only slowly and could re-

43. By "matter" is meant, simply, the "things" in space and time, i.e., in the context of this essay, primarily organisms.
44. Henley, *Murder of Silence*, p. 14.

generate almost over night;[45] destruction, on such terms, could never overtake regeneration. But in nature, destruction is rapid; regeneration is slow.

Similarly for what I have loosely termed "matter," that is, the "collection" of "things" in the world: an environment does not possess an infinite supply of treasure, nor can it ever, cornucopia-like, produce such supplies on demand. There are only so many habitats for rare orchids and giant woodpeckers; once they are gone, Ponthieu's orchid and the ivory-bill are gone with them. The last bear to be seen in the Big Thicket until a few years ago was killed and eaten by the townspeople of Livingston, Texas (in 1953) on the assumption that there were "plenty more where that came from."[46] Those who have killed fish life in area streams through electrical shock, and who have poached frogs and alligators there, act as if the supply were inexhaustible. The same near-sighted assumption doubtless prevented game laws from being enforced in the area until five or six years ago.

Closely allied with what might be termed the Postulate of the Environmental Infinite is the Habit of Inveterate Atomism. In the Thicket now the world's tallest cypress tree may be dying because a thoughtlessly placed road has cut off its water supply. In the same way, the lumber companies' proposed national monument fails to protect the isolated biotic communities precisely because in the monument blueprint they are conceived as spatially isolated and offered no environing protection. A beech forest dies if it is not, *spatially*, surrounded by shade trees. There are no spatially discrete atoms of environment.

Spatial atomism is logically connected with temporal atomism because causal influences preceding from one place to another take time to make themselves felt.[47] There can be no spatial atomism

45. At present it is estimated that the Big Thicket is being cut at the rate of fifty or more acres *a day*. Cf. William O. Douglas, *Farewell to Texas* (New York: McGraw-Hill, 1967), chap. 1.

46. Archer Fullingim, editor of the *Kountze News*, tells an even grimmer horror story. After a great deal of publicity had been expended locally on the ivory-billed woodpecker, a settler walked in and dropped a dead ivory-bill on Fullingim's desk. The man explained that he had shot the bird to make definite identification. There were "plenty more where that one came from," the man drawled. Since then, however, no further ivory-billed woodpeckers have been seen by the man—or by Fullingim.

47. That is, barring some kind of instantaneous "action-at-a-distance."

in nature because changes in one separated place eventually affect the character of other separated places. By temporal atomism I mean the notion that what happens at one moment does not affect the *character* of what happens at successive moments. (In criticizing this concept of temporal atomism, I do not mean to exclude the possibility that there should be temporal atoms in the sense of distinguishable successive temporal "epochs," in Whitehead's terminology.) In natural environments, temporal atomicity in the first sense is a fiction. The insecticides which Rachel Carson describes as being bountifully employed in the Big Thicket[48] are building up slowly in area soils and streams, and in the fatty tissues of higher organisms there; in the future they will kill more fish and bird life than all past poachers could have dreamed. Savannah areas now protected from sporadic grass fires will in the future no longer produce a rich crop of orchids and other herbaceous plants, precisely because occasional burning is a necessary condition of the continued future existence of certain plant communities. Interference with even seemingly insignificant factors at one stage in an ecological succession may have marked effects on the future of that succession, halting it at a subclimax community, derailing it into a disclimax community—or even no community at all.

The present governor of the state of California once remarked: "If you've seen one redwood, you've seen them all." The governor's remark *may* apply satisfactorily to pions and neutrons (and to conservative governors) but it emphatically does not apply to trees, which, on examination, turn out to be distinguishable individuals. The governor's remark, however, is helpful, for it lays bare an unconscious atomism, according to which the "things" in the world are, in themselves, assumed to be identical. We have known for a long time that this is not true of snowflakes, starfish, and fingerprints. Yet we persist in assuming its validity for trees, rivers, and ecosystems.

If this is so it is because we have also denied the possibility that one "thing" should draw its character in any way from the interrelatedness of the other "things" that make its environment; that is, we have denied the possibility that there should be degrees of

48. Rachel Carson, *Silent Spring* (Greenwich, Conn.: Fawcett, 1970), p. 150.

internal relatedness in nature. One tree is different from another not only because it has (or is liable to have) a different genetic structure, but because its development has been conditioned by a different environment. But what is true of individual organisms is still more true of species in their relations to biotic communities. There is a small, white flower (the "beech drop") which grows only under beech groves, and which dies out when the beech are cut. Not only is that flower dependent on the beech grove: its character is defined in terms of its beech grove environs. An animal or plant takes its form and function from the ecological niche it can carve out for itself. Describe an animal and you imply the ecosystem it inhabits; describe a plant community and you can depict what sort of animal can find a niche in it.[49] Recently in the Big Thicket two remarkable insects have been discovered, a new species of "flesh fly" and the "toothpick grasshopper." These can exist only in conjunction with certain insectivorous plants (which in turn can exist only under highly specific soil, water, and climatological conditions).[50] Define one of these insects, and its specific ecosystem is automatically implicated; and conversely. Both logically and in fact, atomism is impossible in environmental situations. Are there, one wonders, really any other kinds of situations?[51]

The end result of our atomism and our infinitism is one which suits our historical penchant for manipulation. By ignoring the interrelations and the natural articulations of biotic communities we have assured ourselves a future of environmental exploitation coupled with expanding economic returns. We have, to use Heidegger's phrase, created a "tool world." Such a world, where resources are infinite and interdependence is nominal at most, cries out for manipulation. But exploitation, manipulation—technology itself—appear from the vantage point of our present crisis to have

49. I do not mean to imply by this that the degree of logical relationship will be the same in every instance. Cases of mutualism and synergism involve closer ties than many other environmental relations. Man, as a "generalized primate," is less bound by *specific* environmental influence than many "over-adapted" species.

50. The toothpick grasshopper, to date, is known to exist only in the Big Thicket; the species of flesh fly discovered there is now known to exist elsewhere.

51. On this point cf. A. N. Whitehead, *Science and the Modern World* (New York: Free Press, 1967), esp. chap. 13, "Requisites for Social Progress."

fundamental limitations. Environmental exploitation occurs not in a void but in an environment, an environment of which the exploiter is a relational part.

It is highly interesting, in retrospect, to note that much of the damage done to the Big Thicket in the past was sanctioned by a "use and possession" law stressing an extremely utilitarian concept of "use" and, therefore, of ownership. Recreational and aesthetic "uses" were rigorously excluded from the framework of legal institutions, primarily in order to sanction exploitation; in turn, the habit of exploitation ruled out any reference to nonmarket values. This bias can hardly be said to have been eradicated from our legal codes—least of all in Texas. Law, Justice Holmes remarked, is the government of the living by the dead.

Between our view of man and our concept of nature there are hidden ties: so much so that our concept of one is almost inevitably the mirror image of the other, at least in important respects.[52] We have viewed nature as infinite, atomistically isolated, and capable of an infinitely extended range of transformations.

There can be no possibility of fully developing here a portrait of the pioneer, the lumberman, the oilfield entrepreneur who so casually wrecked the Big Thicket and similar wilderness areas. (Their psychological lineaments, roughly parallel those of Western industrialists generally.) Such men construed themselves as infinite, at least potentially: capable of transforming an indefinitely extensive space successively into an indefinitely extended future. There would be nothing such a man—or such a mankind—could not do, make, transform, given world enough and time.[53]

It is interesting to note that in the Big Thicket, alongside the backwoodsman and the lumber baron, there exists an Indian culture which has entertained different concepts of man and nature

52. Raymond Williams, "Ideas of Nature," *London Times Literary Supplement*, 4 December 1970, p. 1421.

53. This fundamental article of faith is far from having lost its grip. Cf. for example Richard A. Watson and Patty Jo Watson, *Man and Nature* (New York: Harcourt, Brace and World, 1969), p. 125: "Industrial man is not merely a part of nature, but a part of controlled nature, that is, a part of the physical environment over which man has gained immense control. A step beyond is atomic man, who, through his discovery of a virtually unlimited source of energy, has such powerful control of nature that he can change both men and materials in almost all those mythical ways attributed to the gods, except for changing the laws of nature themselves."

than those of European civilization. In spite of poverty the Alabama and Coushatta tribes refused to allow their timber to be cut; one of the few virgin woodlands in the region covers their original reservation. It was not that the Indians were unable to cut down a tree; after all, steel-bladed axes have been in their possession at least since their encounters with the French in the eighteenth century. Rather, the Indians viewed man as an enjoyer and participator in nature, and nature as possessed of intrinsic value. In his magnificent *Bury My Heart at Wounded Knee*, Dee Brown points out that to the plains Indians it seemed that the white man hated everything in nature, that he killed and destroyed for the sake of it, and not merely so as to be able to survive and live well. One gets the same impression, in retrospect, reflecting on the white backwoodsmen in contrast to the woodland Indians of the South. Different cultures embody different world views; and different world views, as I have been insisting, entail different interactions with nature.

But to return to the majority view under analysis. Man-infinite also viewed himself both in himself and in his projects, atomistically. By this is meant not simply as an atomlike individual over and against other individuals (though this is true enough for many of the pioneer types that settled the Southwest). In the respect that concerns us here it matters not whether one submerges himself in Leviathan or proclaims a state of exemplary anarchy: so long as one proclaims himself *distinct from* nature, whether on religious or technological grounds, he conceives of himself, in this respect, as self-contained, and hence atomlike. Being outside of one's environment means not only that one views himself as if he were *spatially* "outside" his environment, but also as if he were unchanged by environmental changes, and possessed a "nature" uncontaminated by the nature of the things around him. These three assumptions sanction one's disinclination to view one's impingements on nature as interrelated and therefore in need of mutual accommodation. Those who live in the Big Thicket today are in salient respects different from those who have lived elsewhere; the difference in their environment has made them different from the sort of people they would have been had they settled elsewhere. And in transforming their environment they are transforming themselves. For every acre they uproot they unwittingly uproot themselves; every act of negligence toward nature sanctioned or ignored by their religion brings closer the (urban) conditions under which their religious world view can no longer exist.

Beginning with man-infinite, construed atomistically in his relations to nature and in his impingements on it, one ends up with man-pragmatist: at home in, sanctified in, a tool-world of his own making. The world so construed, and man so construed, fit each other exactly; they are perfectly congruent. But if that world does not exist, that man cannot exist. The crisis of the environment engenders a crisis of man.

What, then, is the function of philosophy, in the face of these crises? In a minimal way, this essay has already taken a step toward fulfilling one of these functions. In its negative aspect philosophy acts as a critic of abstractions; and in depicting (however schematically) underlying assumptions which have governed our interaction with environment, this essay has included, almost automatically, a criticism of them. But I would like to hold that philosophy can have a positive function as well, namely, the construction of a world view (including necessarily a man-view or philosophical anthropology) capable of doing coherent justice to the transformed situation in which we find ourselves. Such a world view would have the dual function both of guiding and coordinating our response toward environmental crisis and, on the purely speculative side, of satisfying the desire to know and understand our environment, including ourselves.

One may rightly question how far such a philosophical enterprise might succeed. But it seems clear enough to me that sooner or later it will be tried, and is in fact being attempted by innumerable writers groping with the implication of old attitudes and new problems.[54] Better then that a philosopher make a systematic and disciplined effort.[55] Or at least: that is a philosopher's opportunity.

54. As the most celebrated recent example: Charles A. Reich, *The Greening of America* (New York: Random House, 1970).

55. Such a world view would involve the negation of the schema which has led to environmental misunderstanding and degeneration. In terms of "nature" it would involve the negation of infinitism, whether of space, time, or organisms; it would involve the negation of atomism, whether spatial, temporal or "material," as well as of any supposed "tool world." In terms of man it would involve the denial of infinitude toward and separation from environment, as well as from other men. It would involve the denial of a deeply ingrained "pragmatism." Mechanism, in short, would be negated.

NOTE

A bill to create a Big Thicket Reserve of 84,500 acres was passed unanimously by the United States House of Representatives in December 1973. Both conservationists and, it should be added, large lumber companies, united behind this bill. The United States Senate also passed a bill to create a Big Thicket National Biological Reserve in May 1974.

"Organicism" in some form would, in turn, be affirmed. Perhaps it is time for a greening of the philosophers.

Notes on Contributors

EUGENE ODUM is Alumni Foundation Distinguished Professor of Zoology and Director of the Institute of Ecology at the University of Georgia. A member of the National Academy of Science and Past President of the Ecological Society of America, Professor Odum is the author of numerous papers in professional journals and four books, including his *Fundamentals of Ecology* and *Ecology*. These volumes are widely known throughout the world and have been translated into eight foreign languages.

JOEL FEINBERG is Professor of Philosophy at the Rockefeller University in New York, having previously taught at Brown University, Princeton, and the University of California at Los Angeles. He has received postdoctoral fellowships both from the Center for Advanced Study in the Behavioral Sciences at Stanford and the Harvard University Law School. A frequent contributor to philosophical journals, Professor Feinberg is the author and editor of several books, including *Reason and Responsibility*, *Moral Concepts*, *Doing and Deserving: Essays in the Theory of Responsibility*, and *Abortion*.

WILLIAM T. BLACKSTONE is Professor of Philosophy, former Head of the Department of Philosophy and Religion, and Chairman of the Division of Social Sciences at the University of Georgia. He has contributed numerous articles to philosophical journals and is the author and editor of eight books, including *The Problem of Religious Knowledge*, *Francis Hutcheson and Contemporary Ethical Theory*, *The Concept of Equality*, *Meaning and Existence*, and *Political Philosophy*.

CHARLES HARTSHORNE is presently Professor of Philosophy at the University of Texas, having previously taught at the University of Chicago and Emory University. A former Fulbright Professor at Melbourne University and the Perry Lecturer at Yale University, Hartshorne is a world-renowned process philosopher. The author of numerous essays in philosophical journals, Professor Hartshorne's books include *Reality and Social Process*, *Philosophy and Psychology of Sensation, Man's Vision of God, The Divine Relativity,* and *The Logic of Perfection.*

WALTER H. O'BRIANT is Associate Professor of Philosophy at the University of Georgia. He is the author of several articles in philosophical journals and of a translation and evaluation of Leibniz's *General Investigations Concerning the Analysis of Concepts and Truths.*

NICHOLAS RESCHER is University Professor of Philosophy and Associate Director of the Center for the Philosophy of Science at the University of Pittsburgh. The author of numerous articles in philosophical journals and the editor of the *American Philosophical Quarterly,* Professor Rescher is also the author of twenty books, including *Distributive Justice, Introduction to Value Theory, Studies in Philosophical Analysis,* and *Scientific Explanation.* Professor Rescher has held fellowships and research grants from the Ford Foundation, the Guggenheim Foundation, the American Philosophical Society, the National Science Foundation, and the Carnegie Corporation.

ROBERT G. BURTON is Assistant Professor of Philosophy at the University of Georgia. His special areas of interest are philosophy of science and philosophy of mind. He contributed an essay to the book *Ontological Commitment.*

PETE A. Y. GUNTER is Professor of Philosophy and Chairman of the Department of Philosophy at North Texas State University. The author of a number of articles in philosophical journals and in conservationist journals, Professor Gunter is the editor and translator of *Bergson and the Evolution of Physics* and is the author of *The Big Thicket: A Challenge for Conservation.* He is presently the President of the Big Thicket Association.